Joseph Bellafiore

Author of *English Language Arts*
English Made Easier
Words at Work
Adventures With Words

Essentials
of
English

THIRD EDITION

Dedicated to serving

AMSCO

our nation's youth

When ordering this book, please specify:
either **R 259 H** or ESSENTIALS OF ENGLISH, HARDBOUND

AMSCO SCHOOL PUBLICATIONS, INC.
315 Hudson Street / New York, N.Y. 10013

To Barbara

ISBN 0-87720-678-3

Printed in the United States of America

To the Student

Essentials of English serves to make clear the way in which our living language communicates ideas and experiences between people. If English is your mother tongue, you have already formed certain habits of speaking and writing. Some may be good; others not so good. The material presented here is designed to motivate you to improve your expressional ability by pointing out the acceptable form and the wrong way to say whatever you wish. You will find each topic is well organized with a brief explanation. Then a guiding rule is given with models to follow, and a series of drill exercises to reinforce your learning. The review tests help you to measure your progress.

First and foremost, you must be able to handle the sentence as the unit of thought in order to gain confidence in shaping complete sentences with variety and flexibility. Patterns of sentence structure show you the kinds of sentences that put life and vigor in your letters, compositions, conversations, reports, etc. Grammar tells you more than parts of speech and subject-verb-object; it helps you understand the relation between the parts of a sentence. Spelling rules protect you from careless blunders. Punctuation and capitalization teach you the "traffic signals" important to get your message through to the reader. Vocabulary building develops your sensitivity and awareness in selecting the word that best fits the context.

All together, these essentials of English will guide you and strengthen your power of communication in order to increase your chances for success in your school work, your getting along with others, and your future employment.

Good luck to you!

Cordially yours,
Joseph Bellafiore

Contents

Chapter	Page

PART FOUR

The Final Score

PART ONE

Set the Goalposts

1. USE *STANDARD ENGLISH*

The field of English has definite goalposts in handling language. You may find these goalposts by noticing the current usage of cultivated speakers and writers and by looking in the dictionary. Avoid running out-of-bounds when you are carrying the ball. Learn the limits of play and you escape penalty.

Standard English is the way educated people speak and write. "Direct, clear, forceful expression is a reflection of clean and uncluttered thinking." (U.S. Commissioner of Education)

Nonstandard English violates the rules of grammar and usage. Avoid such errors as "I ain't done nothin" and "You should of went home." Better say, "I haven't done anything" and "You should have gone home." Whether you are a native here or a newcomer from another country, you must acquire a satisfactory level of written and spoken English. You are preparing yourself for higher education, a worthwhile career, and the courtesies of social living.

Mark Twain once said, "The difference between the right word and another word is the difference between lightning and a lightning bug." The power of language is enormous. Carelessness or fuzziness of language shows poor or sloppy thinking. Therefore, use standard English to fit the time and place and person that the situation requires.

2. MEASURE YOUR WRITING BY THE SELF-CHECKING SCALE

Writing is not easy. First you must gather your thoughts, using your experience and imagination. Then you must put them down in good order and correct English. To do these two things well, you must work. You have to develop an openness in sharing ideas and feelings. You must also build better sentences with correct spelling and punctuation.

How can you measure your writing? After your teacher rates a set of papers and gives them back in class, you may exchange yours with your classmates. Notice the faults and merits. Reading papers aloud for comment helps, too. The greatest benefit comes from personal chats with your teacher. For your own guidance, use this *Self-Checking Scale*. Be honest in finding your weaknesses and try your best to improve your writing. Practice makes perfect!

SELF-CHECKING SCALE

Do you use *good* English, or are you guilty of *poor* English?

GOOD ENGLISH	POOR ENGLISH
A. Clean-cut sentences with complete thoughts	Incomplete sentences, or run-on rambling ideas
B. Correct grammar showing clear thinking	Faulty grammar making vague thought-connections
C. Proper choice of words to express meaning	Careless misuse of words or aimless repeating
D. Careful observance of the basic rules of spelling and punctuation	Disregard of the essentials of spelling and punctuation
E. Lively variety in sentence structure and diction	Deadly sameness in the way you express ideas

3. TAKE AN EYE-OPENING QUIZ

Before the doctor gives you a prescription, he or she looks you over. The doctor may check your pulse and temperature. So too, before asking you to study, your teacher may test you to find out what you need to learn.

This quiz covers many of the essentials of English: sentence structure, grammar, spelling, and punctuation. Take time to read carefully and avoid plain guessing. Ready?

Directions: Select the correct sentence in each pair below.

1*a*. You shouldn't have done that.
  b. You shouldn't have did that.

2*a*. It's not raining anymore.
  b. Its not raining anymore.

3*a*. The cause of all their troubles and cares were ended.
  b. The cause of all their troubles and cares was ended.

4*a*. Being that she was late, she ran for the bus.
  b. Since she was late, she ran for the bus.

5*a*. We couldn't hardly hear the music.
  b. We could hardly hear the music.

6*a*. After winning the title, he didn't try anything else.
  b. After winning the title, he didn't try nothing else.

7*a*. Watching the parade before the football game, the floats came into view.
  b. Watching the parade before the football game, we viewed the floats.

8*a*. They preferred comedies on TV, not stories of crime and violence.
  b. They preferred comedies on TV. Not stories of crime and violence.

9*a*. Strolling along the beach and collecting seashells.
  b. She was strolling along the beach and collecting seashells.

10*a*. The tailor pressed the pants, the customer returned them and complained of creases.
  b. The tailor pressed the pants. The customer returned them and complained of creases.

11*a*. He apologized for accidently loosening one of the buttons.
  b. He apologized for accidentally loosening one of the buttons.

12*a*. School cafeterias should have soundproof walls and ceilings.
  b. School cafeterias should have soundproof walls and cielings.

13*a*. Wordsworth wrote, "Our birth is but a sleep and a forgetting."
  b. Wordsworth wrote, "Our birth is but a sleep and a forgeting."

14*a*. The coffee stains seemed barely noticeable on the tablecloth.
  b. The coffee stains seemed barely noticable on the tablecloth.

15*a*. Our country has welcomed many foriegners to our shores.
  b. Our country has welcomed many foreigners to our shores.

16*a*. How could you say that Tina is taller than her?
  b. How could you say that Tina is taller than she?

17*a*. After all is said and done, there is no excuse for overeating.
  b. After all is said and done there is no excuse for overeating.

18*a*. Precious metals have advanced in price: gold, silver, platinum.
  b. Precious metals have advanced in price, gold, silver, platinum.

19*a*. To avoid gossip, everyone should mind their own business.
  b. To avoid gossip, everyone should mind his or her own business.

20*a*. In her last game of tennis, she played really well.
  b. In her last game of tennis, she played real good.

4. CHECK YOUR ANSWERS AND STUDY THE REASONS FOR THE CORRECT ANSWERS

1a. The correct use of the principal parts of the verb *do* requires the past participle *done*, not the past tense *did*.

2a. *It's* is a contracted form of *It is*. The use of *Its*, a pronoun, is a mistake caused by similar sound.

3b. Agreement between subject and verb requires the singular verb *was* after the singular subject *cause*.

4b. *Since* is acceptable, but *Being that* is nonstandard. *Because* may also be used in place of *Being that*.

5b. *Hardly* is a negative adverb (like *scarcely*, *barely*) and may not be used with *not*. Avoid the double negative in *a*.

6a. Avoid the double negative in *b* (did*n't* . . . *no*thing). Another way to say this is: ". . . he tried nothing else."

7b. The subject is *we* ("viewed the floats"). Avoid the dangling participle in *a* ("Watching . . . game, the floats came into view").

8a. This is a complete sentence. Avoid the fragment given as a sentence in *b*.

9b. This is a complete sentence. Avoid the fragment given as a sentence in *a*.

10b. These are two sentences. Avoid the run-on blunder in *a*, which uses a comma followed by a small letter instead of a period followed by a capital letter.

11b. Correct spelling of *accidentally* is given here. Avoid the misspelling given in *a*.

12a. Correct spelling of *ceilings* is given here. Avoid the misspelling given in *b*.

13a. Correct spelling of *forgetting* is given here. Avoid the misspelling given in *b*.

14a. Correct spelling of *noticeable* is given here. Avoid the misspelling given in *b*.

15b. Correct spelling of *foreigners*. Avoid the misspelling given in *a*.

16b. Use the nominative case *she* after a comparative *than*.

17a. Correct punctuation shown by *comma* after an introductory clause.

18a. Correct punctuation shown by *colon* to introduce a series of nouns.

19b. The word *everyone* is singular and is correctly followed by *his or her*.

20a. The kind of playing requires adverbs: *really well*. Avoid using adjectives (*real good*) to describe how she played tennis.

PART TWO

Make Sentences That Carry Ideas

Sentence comes from Latin, meaning "to think or to feel." A sentence expresses in words whatever you want to tell or ask someone. Human beings have other ways of communicating with one another: by gestures, signals, musical notes, colors (red means danger), sounds (sirens are alarms), and so on. But, the sentence makes a direct person-to-person contact in as few words or as many words as are necessary.

The main point about a sentence is this: it must make sense! Remember this definition: "A sentence is a group of words so related as to convey a complete thought." Do you get the idea?

Take a look at these word groups. Can you select the ones which are acceptable sentences?

1. Help!
2. What's wrong?
3. Somebody fell into the pool.
4. Call the lifeguard!
5. Here she comes on the run.

Answer: All are acceptable because they make complete sense.

Chapter 1

Putting Together the Parts of a Sentence

WHAT IS A SENTENCE?

A *sentence* is a group of words so related as to convey a complete thought.
Take that definition and scramble the words around and you lose the meaning: "A complete thought so related as a sentence is a group of words to convey." Why is this fuzzy? It has the same words but the wrong order.

Putting together the parts of a sentence requires clear thinking and careful assembling of ideas, just as putting together the pieces of a jigsaw puzzle makes the picture clear.

Can you take the following scrambled blocks of words and rearrange them to make a sentence with good sense?

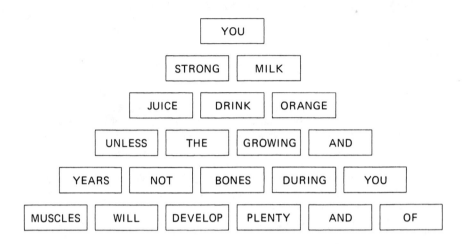

The right words in the right order are: "Unless you drink plenty of milk and orange juice during the growing years, you will not develop strong bones and muscles."

Exercise—Putting Words Together in Order to Make Sense

Rearrange these groups of words into acceptable sentences.

1. fish keep tank die so water not clean the that the will
2. we hat scarf pipe snowman with a made and a
3. the runner the pitcher the ball home plate to tossed to catch
4. get extra money savings your interest banks put in to
5. short take after walk I like to lunch a quick a
6. sometimes we breaks come bus down school and late to the
7. your smile brush if you will brighter be your teeth
8. the city the lights when looks go on wonderland a like
9. pie frozen fresh fruit homemade with beats any kind a
10. someone else before why first facts blame you not the get

SUBJECT AND PREDICATE OF A SENTENCE

A sentence is a group of words arranged to convey meaning from one person to another. No matter how short or how long a sentence may be, it can always be divided into two parts: the *subject* and the *predicate*. Notice how these basic parts of a sentence may be enlarged by adding other words, yet the sentence keeps its two main parts:

SUBJECT	PREDICATE
Fish _____	*swim.*
Some *fish* _____	*swim* vertically.
Some pet *fish* _____	*swim* vertically as well as horizontally.

Now, in every one of these sentences you can see that:

1. The subject is *fish*, the thing we are speaking about.
2. The predicate is *swim*, the verb that tells what the thing is doing.

DEFINITION OF SUBJECT

The *simple subject* is the word or words used to name the person, place, or thing we are speaking about in a sentence.

The *druggist* filled the prescription. (one word)
The *house* and the *driveway* face the busy street. (two words)

In each sentence, the subject tells whom or what we are talking about. The subject is the doer.

DEFINITION OF VERB

The *predicate verb* is the word or words used to describe the action or tell what the subject does.

The students *wrote* letters to their pen pals.
(*Wrote* is a verb.)

A *verb phrase* includes two or more words.

You *should save* some of your money.
(*Should save* is a verb phrase.)

HOW TO FIND THE SUBJECT AND VERB

In order to find the subject of a sentence, ask yourself this question: *"What or whom are we speaking about?"* In the following examples, the subject is underlined once.

Whom or what are we speaking about?

The <u>captain</u> steered the ship across the ocean.
<u>Springtime</u> fills us with new hope.

To find the verb, ask yourself: *"What is the person or thing doing?"* In the following examples, the subject is underlined once, the verb twice.

What is this person or thing doing?

The <u>father</u> <u>fed</u> the baby a bottle of fresh milk.
     S   V

The <u>snow</u> <u>has covered</u> the roads.
    S   V

Exercise—Subject and Verb

In each of the following sentences, write the subject in one column and the verb in a second column.

1. My father, tired and ill, went to bed early.
2. The manager of the team praised his players.
3. Slowly the water dripped from the roof.
4. The squirrel, frightened by the noise, ran up the tree.
5. The old man with his dog braved the storm.
6. Fred has gone to school.
7. The driver of the bus sounded his horn.
8. The boy, cold and hungry, sat by the fireplace.
9. Suddenly we heard a loud cry.
10. We turned out the lights before leaving the house.
11. You should have gone to the game with us.
12. The little girl with the doll is my niece.
13. Nervously he opened the letter.
14. The child, scolded by his mother, cried bitterly.
15. My teacher of English is Miss Borelli.
16. That tall boy was elected captain of the baseball team.
17. My French book got wet in the rain.
18. I studied hard before taking the test.
19. You should have seen him dancing.
20. The man with the mustache is Joe's father.

MORE ABOUT THE SUBJECT AND VERB

The subject may be near the beginning, the middle, or the end of a sentence.

Quickly, everyone ran from the burning building.

After the rain, the game resumed until dark.

Down the hill rolled the disabled car.

The subject may have two or more parts.

Boys and girls attend our school.

John and I built the wagon.

Mary, Jane, and Alice are sisters.

The verb may also have two or more parts.

I will call or write you soon.

Tony fell but laughed over the incident.

The children ran and played for an hour.

Sometimes the subject is understood (not mentioned).

Give me the book.

In the above sentence, the word *give* is the verb. The subject is *you*. The sentence would read if written in full:

(You) give me the book.

Note that in a question the subject comes between the parts of a verb phrase.

Have the pigeons flown away?

Will your friends go to the game?

Make Sentences That Carry Ideas 9

Exercise—Subject and Verb

In each of the following sentences, write the subject in one column and the verb in a second column.

1. Out of the cage flew the bird.
2. Have the children dressed and eaten?
3. Drink your milk.
4. Very carefully she wrapped the package.
5. Inside the house all was quiet.
6. Will you write me soon?
7. Tell me about it.
8. Louise, Alice, and Jane sang and danced all day.
9. May Harriet and I go on the boat ride?
10. At the corner of Main and State Streets we met Joyce.
11. Father and Mother must have gone to the show.
12. Bob and Joe walked home from school.
13. Have you seen Elsa recently?
14. Fortunately the door was strong.
15. Frances and I talked and then went for a walk.
16. Will you go to the store for me?
17. In the park we met Jackie and Danielle.
18. Suddenly it started to rain.
19. Shall we ride or walk?
20. Beside the house stood a car.

HOW A SENTENCE GROWS

A sentence always contains two basic parts: a subject and a verb. A sentence grows by the addition of other parts called *modifiers*. **A *modifier* is an element used in a sentence to qualify the meaning.** A modifier may be a word, a phrase, or a clause.

MODIFIERS: WORDS, PHRASES, CLAUSES

For example, the *wind* may be described as a "*gentle* breeze" or a "*furious* wind." These WORDS qualify the meaning by telling us whether the wind is balmy or violent.

There are PHRASES that tell us about the wind: "warm winds *from the south*" or "icy blasts *from the north*."

And there are CLAUSES to describe the wind: "It's an ill wind *that blows no good*."

USING MODIFIERS TO BUILD SENTENCES

A bare sentence stands like a tree in winter with its trunk and branches stripped. To avoid that empty look, add a few modifiers (words, phrases, or clauses) that will give the sentence clearer shape and fuller meaning.

BARE: Television gives the news.

                        S   V

ADD A WORD: Television gives the *important* news.

ADD A PHRASE: Television gives the important news *of the day*.

ADD A CLAUSE: Television gives the important news of the day *as it happens*.

As you can see, the sentence stands firmly on its subject and verb, but the added parts round out the meaning.

Exercise—Modifiers

This exercise is a bit tricky! Put together a word, a phrase, and a clause to form a complete sentence. Of course, you will add a subject and a predicate. As a model, we provide an answer to the first group.

MODEL: 1. It was *delightful* to walk *in the morning while everybody slept*.

WORDS	PHRASES	CLAUSES
1. delightful	in the morning	while everybody slept
2. worn out	without any heels	since the ten-mile hike
3. bitterly	after swallowing	as the doctor had ordered
4. officially	next to the curb	which had a NO PARKING sign
5. uselessly	about his excuses	although the judge fined him
6. angrily	at the storekeeper	because the price was too high

Exercise—Writing Original Sentences

Here is a list of interesting ways of making up your own sentences. Try some or all of these suggestions! Feel free to modify any of them to suit your ideas.

A. *Write original sentences answering these questions:*

1. Why do the birds fly southward before winter?
2. Why can you hear the sea when you put a shell next to your ear?
3. How do you make new friends?

B. *Write original sentences about clothes and appearance:*

4. Is it important to follow fashion?
5. Do you favor a dress code?
6. Are boots and raincoats necessary when it rains?

C. *Write original sentences dealing with current affairs:*

7. What was the most important news event this week?
8. Which side of a recent local issue did you take?
9. Why is there always a certain percentage of persons out of work?

D. *Write original sentences about personal problems:*

10. How much allowance a week should you get?
11. What chores should you be asked to do?
12. How can you choose a worthwhile occupation or career?

E. *Write original sentences using these ideas about sports and games:*

13. only two minutes left to play
14. a ball coming right toward the batter
15. jumping over the last tackler near the goal

F. *Write original sentences using some of these ideas to describe your favorite radio or television programs:*

16. preference for comedy, mystery, or adventure
17. popular dance bands and folksingers
18. commercials as entertaining or boring interruptions

G. *Write original sentences using these ideas related to school:*

19. finding a lost sneaker in the locker room
20. handing in some report a week late
21. raising your hand to volunteer in class

H. *Write original sentences based on your personal experiences as suggested by the following ideas:*

22. a trip to the park, the zoo, a museum, etc.
23. my most memorable birthday celebration
24. meeting the new neighbors on our block

I. *Write original sentences using these clauses as part of the complete statements or questions you prepare:*

25. if I ever get another pet
26. after the relatives and friends left the party
27. where the pool becomes nine feet deep

Chapter 2

Identifying the Kinds of Sentences and Clauses

A. KINDS OF SENTENCES

There are four kinds of sentences according to your purpose. You may *state a fact, ask a question, give an order*, or *express strong emotion*. Notice the different ways these sentences deliver their message:

KIND	PURPOSE	SENTENCE
declarative:	states a fact	Here comes Tom.
interrogative:	asks a question	Is Nina coming here?
imperative:	gives an order	Come here, Theresa.
exclamatory:	shows strong emotion	Hurrah! Sarah is coming!

Why learn these? To encourage you to use them for variety and change of pace! If you take a look at one of your own paragraphs or letters, you will probably find that 99 percent of all your sentences are declarative statements. For a bit of interesting variation, try to use some of the other kinds. Instead of starting your next composition with the usual straightforward topic sentence, change to a question, a command, or an exclamation. Compare these:

> We enjoyed ourselves very much at the game. (*declarative*)
> What a time we had at the game! (*exclamatory*)
> Will we ever forget that game? (*interrogative*)
> Let's enjoy ourselves at the game. (*imperative*)

Once you become aware of these variations, you will observe their being widely used in newspaper ads and television commercials:

> Fly now, pay later!
> Come on down (to Miami)!
> Why settle for less?
> Chew your little troubles away.
> Do you suffer from head colds?

Exercise—Kinds of Sentences

Classify the following sentences as *declarative* (DECL.), *interrogative* (INT.), *imperative* (IMP.), or *exclamatory* (EXCL.).

1. We have been waiting for the bus for twenty minutes.
2. Tell her she will have to explain to her mother how it happened.
3. May I write my name on the cast on your arm?
4. Plants need sunshine and lots of water.
5. If you have a slight headache, take an aspirin.
6. The passenger looked suspicious as he approached the pilot.
7. "Fly the plane to Cuba!" the skyjacker demanded.
8. This is the best car for the lowest price.
9. I am a doctor, not a coal miner!
10. Turn down the radio; it is too loud.
11. While the captain is asleep, I am in command!
12. Shall we paint the stage set outselves to save expenses?
13. He was a tall man, over six feet tall, and broad-chested.
14. I could tell they were coming by the sound of their voices.
15. Then we heard one horrid, long-drawn scream.
16. Does she wear this brand of perfume?
17. He filled a pipe and sat silently puffing away.
18. Captain Flint was the bloodthirstiest buccaneer that ever sailed!
19. Afloat at sea, I now began to be tortured by the sun!
20. Give first aid until the ambulance arrives.
21. Since you are well prepared, you should not worry about passing the final exam.
22. While Ida parked the car, I bought the tickets.
23. If prices continue to rise, shoppers will buy less.
24. The President lost reelection because voters blamed him for the high unemployment.
25. A raggedly dressed man approached me and asked for money.

B. CLAUSES

DEFINITIONS

A *clause* is a group of words containing a subject and a predicate.

There are two kinds of clauses: *main clause* and *subordinate clause*. The essential difference is that a main clause can stand by itself and make sense, but a subordinate clause cannot make sense alone.

A *main clause* is a group of words containing a subject and a predicate and makes sense when standing alone. (Also called an *independent clause*.)

> Doug rowed the boat.
> Janet felt happy again.
> We won the contest.

A *subordinate clause* is a group of words that contains a subject and a predicate but depends on the main clause to complete its meaning. (Also called a *dependent clause*.)

_____ unless it stops raining.	
_____ when she found her purse.	The main clause is
Because traffic was heavy, _____ .	missing in each group.
If you study hard, _____ .	

By adding main clauses, we obtain these complete thoughts:

We will not leave the house unless it stops raining.
  main clause   subordinate clause

Iris breathed easier when she found her purse.
  main clause   subordinate clause

Because traffic was heavy, we were late for the game.
  subordinate clause   main clause

If you study hard, you will get good grades.
  subordinate clause   main clause

A subordinate clause is introduced by a *subordinate conjunction*. In the above clauses, *unless*, *when*, *because*, and *if* are examples.

A *subordinate conjunction* is a word or group of words used to connect a subordinate clause to another part of the sentence.

A subordinate conjunction shows the relationship in meaning between the subordinate clause it introduces and the word that it modifies. Some often used subordinate conjunctions are

after	before	provided that	when
although	despite the fact that	since	where
as	even though	though	whether
as well as	if	unless	while
because	in order that	until	why

Other words, called *relative pronouns*, that serve to introduce a subordinate clause are *who* (or *whom*), *that*, *which*.

Exercise—Main and Subordinate Clauses

Copy each of the following sentences. Identify the main clause, and if there is one, the subordinate clause.

1. We had a quick lunch of hamburgers and shakes before we went to the movies.
2. This is the house that my grandparents lived in.
3. If you are in doubt about the spelling of a word, you should consult a dictionary.
4. Louise invited me for dinner tomorrow.
5. In the morning during vacations, I jog around the lake.
6. Canada is to the north of the United States, while Mexico is to the south.
7. I finished the last problem just as the bell rang.
8. What a cold day it was!
9. Dan will eat chicken, although he much prefers steak.
10. When she heard the good news, she just smiled.

Exercise—Changing Subordinate Clauses into Sentences

Change each subordinate clause into a sentence by connecting it to a main clause.

INCOMPLETE: when you pay the bill
COMPLETE: When you pay the bill, *be sure to count the change.*

INCOMPLETE: because rainfall was meager
COMPLETE: *Farmers had a poor crop* because rainfall was meager.

1. because we cannot trust them
2. since the air conditioner was out of order
3. while the guests were playing bridge
4. if you buy a chance in the lottery
5. as soon as the whistle blew
6. which was just the kind of thing she always wanted
7. although his father had tried to put it together
8. unless you are willing to practice every day
9. even though the questions covered the material studied
10. when the rivers flood in springtime

USES OF CLAUSES

What is the business of clauses? Since a clause has a subject and predicate, it can serve in several ways to convey meaning.

(*a*) A SINGLE MAIN CLAUSE forms a *simple* sentence.

> I enjoy window shopping.
> Alaska is our largest state.
> May I have another sandwich?

(*b*) A MAIN CLAUSE + A MAIN CLAUSE form a *compound* sentence.

> Anne studied to be a nurse, and Larry took a job as a salesman.
> main clause   main clause

> Shall we meet at the movies, or will you call me first?
> main clause   main clause

> He wanted to become a musician, but he became a banker.
> main clause   main clause

Main clauses are connected by a *coordinate conjunction*. Examples are *and*, *or*, and *but*, as in the sentences above.

A *coordinate conjunction* is a word used to connect main clauses in a sentence. The most common ones are *and*, *or*, *but*.

(*c*) A MAIN CLAUSE + A SUBORDINATE CLAUSE form a *complex* sentence. (The subordinate conjunctions are italicized in the sentences below.)

> *When* the light changes, traffic moves.
> subordinate clause   main clause

> The baby fell asleep *after* he had eaten.
> main clause   subordinate clause

> *If* you are invited, will you join our club?
> subordinate clause   main clause

SUMMARY

- SIMPLE SENTENCE: one main clause—
  You can lose weight.

- COMPOUND SENTENCE: two or more main clauses—
  You can lose weight *and* you will stay healthy
  but you must choose proper foods.

- COMPLEX SENTENCE: main clause + subordinate clause—
  You can lose weight *if* you choose proper foods.

Exercise—Kinds of Sentences

Classify the following sentences by writing S for simple sentence, Cx for complex sentence, and Cd for compound sentence.

Observe two cautions:

1. *Do not confuse a compound verb with a compound sentence.*

> He *entered* the room and *took* his seat.
> (This is a simple sentence. It has two verbs but only one main clause.)

> He entered the room, and then he took his seat.
> (This is a compound sentence because it has two main clauses.)

2. *Do not confuse a phrase with a clause.*

> After lunch I started my composition.
> (This is a simple sentence. It has only a main clause.)

> After I had eaten lunch, I started my composition.
> (This is a complex sentence consisting of a subordinate clause and a main clause.)

1. I always go to bed early.
2. While I was talking to Jack, I saw Robert walking with Mary.
3. Some people like football, but others prefer hockey, a thrilling sport.
4. Slowly and quietly she made her way to the door, but no one was there.
5. Richard and Alfred ate their dinner and went to the show.
6. The problems were difficult, but I was able to solve them.
7. After the long walk in the park, we stopped for refreshments.
8. Tom, my friend and classmate, lives across the street from me.
9. Mr. Brown is the teacher whom I admire most.
10. With the money, I'll buy skates and a bike.
11. We had better take a taxi, or we will be late for the play.
12. We'll not be able to get into the concert unless we buy tickets in advance.
13. "Should we entertain the children at home, or should we take them to the amusement park?" Mother asked.
14. Where did you find the book?
15. From the top of the tree, we had a clear view of the lake.
16. This is an interesting story, and you should read it.
17. I went to the store which my uncle owns.
18. Just as I started to type my report, the lights went out.
19. Where are you going?
20. I came home early and cooked dinner.
21. It is better to be honest in everything.
22. We lived in Albany for ten years and then moved to Dallas.
23. As we were walking home, it started to rain.

24. There is no place like home, according to the song.
25. John ate hurriedly and then went to the concert.
26. "Where are you going so late at night when you have a test tomorrow?" Mother inquired.
27. After school we took a long walk in the park.
28. Henry will go to the store, and you will study your chemistry.
29. During the night we were awakened by an explosion.
30. I will go to the game if my father gives me the money.
31. From where we sat in the stadium, we could see every play.
32. Slowly and cautiously she opened the package.
33. When I opened the door, the dog rushed in.
34. I visited my aunt in Chicago last summer, and I will visit her again this summer.
35. "Will you wait with me at the airport until my plane takes off?" Donna asked.

COMBINING SENTENCES

Make it your business to learn how to write interesting and varied sentences, as illustrated below. Take a little time to link the ideas together!

GROUP I	
Babyish	*Simple Sentence*
I gave Richard a birthday gift. It was a sweater. It was a blue and red sweater.	I gave Richard a blue and red sweater as a birthday gift.

GROUP II	
Babyish	*Compound Sentence*
We didn't go on a picnic. It rained all day. We are planning to go next week.	Owing to the rain we didn't go on a picnic, but we are planning to go next week.

GROUP III	
Babyish	*Complex Sentence*
Helen was late. She was hurrying to school. She lost her ring.	While hurrying to school because she was late, Helen lost her ring.

Exercise—Combining Sentences

Two or three short sentences may be changed into a single sentence by combining clauses. For example:

TWO: He was very strong. He could lift a table.
ONE: He was so strong that he could lift a table.

1. She walked to the center of the stage.
   The orchestra started to play her song.

2. They ran to catch the bus.
   The bus stopped at the traffic light.

3. Tony drew an original poster for the art contest.
   The theme was "Love thy neighbor."

4. The warm sun melted the ice on the pond.
   The attendant put up a "NO SKATING ALLOWED" sign.

5. Growing youngsters need plenty of good food.
   Their bodies will develop strong and healthy.

6. There was nobody in sight.
   He knocked carefully on the front door.
   The lights went out inside.

7. Mary put a dollar a week in her savings account.
   The bank paid regular interest.
   At Christmas she bought presents for her family.

8. Ellen cut the clams up for bait.
   She put the bait on the fishhook.
   She quickly snared a striped bass.

9. Fred tried a long shot across the court.
   The ball bounced off the rim of the basket.
   He ran in and recovered the ball.

10. Barbara cut the material to make a skirt.
    She sewed the hem on the machine.
    She stitched the zipper in by hand.

Chapter 3

Building Better Sentence Patterns

BASIC SENTENCE PATTERNS

For clear expression of ideas, words are ordinarily arranged in these three sentence patterns:

- **S-V** (subject + verb)

  1. Stock prices advanced.
          s   v
  2. Rare coins cost more.
         s   v
  3. Butter melts.
       s   v

  4. Virtue triumphs.
        s   v
  5. The memory lingers on.
         s   v

- **S-V-O** (subject + verb + object)

  6. The customer paid the bill.
         s   v   o
  7. The officer arrested the suspect.
         s   v   o
  8. An accident slowed traffic.
         s   v   o

  9. A big tree shaded the lawn.
         s   v   o
  10. The diver found a pearl.
         s   v   o

- **S-LV-N** (subject + linking verb + noun)
  or
- **S-LV-ADJ** (subject + linking verb + adjective)

  11. Sid was captain.
        S LV   N
  12. Hours appeared years.
        s   LV   N
  13. The soup became watery.
         S   LV   ADJ

  14. The stars seemed brighter.
         S   LV   ADJ
  15. Eva looked puzzled.
        S   LV   ADJ

ACTION AND LINKING VERBS

An *action verb* expresses action. It tells what the *subject is doing*.

The cup <u>dropped</u> to the floor.

          action

Flames <u>spread</u> through the building.

        action

Did you <u>write</u> a letter to the radio station?

        action

A *linking verb* describes a condition related to the subject. The most common linking verb is *to be* and its various forms: *am, is, are, was, were,* etc. Other linking verbs are *seem, grow, appear, look, feel, smell, sound, stay, remain, taste.*

Frank <u>is</u> my next-door neighbor.

S   linking

Ocean air <u>smells</u> salty.

   S   linking

Caution: Some linking verbs may also be action verbs, according to how they are used in sentences.

I <u>feel</u> too tired to bowl this afternoon.

S linking

<u>Feel</u> the bark of the tree.

action

COMPLEMENTS OF THE VERB

A complement is a word used to *complete* the meaning of a verb. There are three kinds of complements:

***Direct object:* a noun or pronoun that names the receiver of the action of the verb.**

The Governor signed the <u>bill</u> into law.

     S   v   o

The bank cashed the <u>check</u> promptly.

   S   v   o

Predicate noun: **a noun that follows a linking verb and refers to the same person as the subject.**

Washington became our first <u>president</u>.
   S   LV   N

The manager of the store was once a <u>clerk</u>.
  S   LV   N

Predicate adjective: **an adjective that follows a linking verb and tells something about the subject.**

Your excuse sounds <u>unbelievable</u>.
     S   LV   ADJ

Edna appeared <u>sorry</u> for spilling the milk.
 S   LV   ADJ

Exercise—Basic Sentence Patterns

Sentence Pattern I. Identify the subject and the verb: S-V.

EXAMPLE: Mother went to the store.
                 S   V

1. The dog ran away from its owner.
2. The ground froze during the winter.
3. The old stone wall collapsed after the thaw.
4. In the evening the stars appear in the sky.
5. At last, the ship's anchor dropped into the bay.

Sentence Pattern II. Identify the subject, the verb, and the object: S-V-O.

EXAMPLE: The next batter hit a homer.
                      S   V   O

6. After the game, the two captains shook hands.
7. The alert cashier pushed the hidden alarm.
8. The weary shopper searched the store for her handbag.
9. Despite the high wind, the ferry made a safe landing.
10. In case of a tie, both contestants receive the award.

Sentence Pattern III. Identify the subject, the linking verb, and the predicate noun (S-LV-N) or predicate adjective (S-LV-ADJ).

EXAMPLES: My new neighbor is a musician.
                       S   LV   N

                  The children grew tired.
                     S   LV ADJ

11. At midnight the coach became a pumpkin again.
12. The fair-haired girl seemed an angel on the stage.
13. Her elbow appeared bruised from the fall.
14. The prisoners of war were really boys in uniform.
15. The fishes actually looked silvery in the moonlight.

HOW TO ENLARGE THE BASIC SENTENCE PATTERNS

You can build up the basic sentence patterns by adding words, phrases, or clauses. Compare the fullness of the following sentences, 1–15, with those we studied on page 21.

S-V (subject + verb).

1. Stock prices advanced.
   Late in the afternoon, stock prices of airlines advanced.
2. Rare coins cost more.
   Rare coins cost more because they are hard to get.
3. Butter melts.
   Butter on hot pancakes melts quickly on contact.
4. Virtue triumphs.
   Although wrongdoing exists, virtue often triumphs.
5. The memory lingers on.
   The party is over, but the memory lingers on.

S-V-O (subject + verb + object)

6. The customer paid the bill.
   When the customer got the package, he paid the bill.
7. The officer arrested the suspect.
   The wary officer promptly arrested the suspect.
8. An accident slowed traffic.
   An accident caused by a trailer truck slowed the bridge traffic.
9. A big tree shaded the lawn.
   A big oak tree planted years ago shaded the lawn in the yard.
10. The diver found a pearl.
    The deep-sea diver found a perfect pearl off Bermuda.

S-LV-N   (subject + linking verb + noun)

or

S-LV-ADJ   (subject + linking verb + adjective)

11. Sid was captain.
    My friend Sid was captain of last year's team.
12. Hours appeared years.
    While I was waiting for the dentist, the hours appeared years.
13. The soup became watery.
    The chicken soup with noodles became quite watery.
14. The stars seemed brighter.
    In the mountains the stars seemed brighter in August.
15. Eva looked puzzled.
    Little Baby Eva looked puzzled when the doll started walking.

HOW TO AVOID FAULTY SENTENCES

Do your compositions come back to you with red ink suggestions by your teacher? Are your sentences awkward? skimpy? overstuffed? Take the corrections in the right spirit as a helpful guide for improving your writing. If you have faulty sentences, learn a better way of expressing your ideas. Study the following kinds of weak or ineffective sentences and notice how to improve them.

I. Skimpy Sentences

Faulty	*Better*
• Short, meager, disconnected ideas.	• Combine short sentences into a longer pattern showing connection.
We arrived late. We went to bed. We ate no supper.	Arriving late, we went to bed without eating supper.

Exercise—How to Improve Faulty Sentences

Following the previous suggestion, rewrite these faulty sentences in clear, acceptable form.

1. She cut the cookies. She baked them. She took some for lunch.
2. The fog lifted. The sun came out. It was getting clear on the bay.
3. The lights flickered. They went out. It was a power failure.

4. We smelled gas. Mother phoned the gas company. A technician came.
5. He helped with the dishes. He washed them. Then she dried them.

II. Wrong Connections

Faulty	Better
• Poor subordination of ideas; the parts are not linked together properly.	• Use logical connecting words to show the proper relation between ideas, whether main or subordinate.
Another activity where you have to match wits is if you join the Chess and Checkers Club.	When you wish to match wits, another activity to join is the Chess and Checkers Club.

Exercise

6. Although I wore my green tie and new brown suit, it was sleeting yesterday.
7. Less crime and violence will occur when guns must be registered while mail order purchases will have to be stopped.
8. Cream puffs are easy to make with crispy shells that you stuff with whipped cream, and you cover them with chocolate syrup.
9. The astronauts circled the moon and returned to earth when the President sent them a congratulatory message.
10. The lady at the corner house had offered the boys two dollars for clearing the snow off the sidewalk, and they asked for three dollars as it took them two hours.

III. Dangling Modifiers

Faulty	Better
• Wrong position of a modifier in a sentence makes the meaning unclear or ridiculous.	• Put the modifier near the word it describes.
Tom wanted a harmonica from the music store having chrome-plated sides.	Tom wanted a harmonica having chrome-plated sides from the music store.

• Faulty identification of the subject makes the meaning ridiculous.	• Reconstruct the sentence to make the subject clear and sensible.
Strolling along the riverside, the bridge came into view. (Who did the strolling?)	While I was strolling along the riverside, the bridge came into view. or:
	Strolling along the riverside, I saw the bridge.

Exercise

11. Putting her hand into her purse, the car keys fell out.
12. He bought the used car from an old friend with spare snow tires.
13. Climbing up the stairs, the rug came loose and he fell.
14. Running after the bus, the bus squealed to a stop and we just made it.
15. The sanitation workers collected the garbage from the homeowner scattered along the curb.

IV. Lacking Parallel Structure

Faulty	*Better*
• Wrong shift in form for similar ideas.	• Keep similar ideas in parallel form.
I like swimming, hiking, and to fish.	I like swimming, hiking, and fishing.
(2 nouns and 1 infinitive)	(3 nouns) or:
	I like to swim, hike, and fish.
	(3 infinitives)

Exercise

16. She promised to take care of him in sickness and when he was healthy, too.
17. The child grew in size and strength, and also grew in wisdom.
18. She had many talents for show business because she could sing, dance, act, and used to tell jokes.
19. My cousin likes to collect rare coins, unusual stamps, and goes after strange rocks and minerals.
20. Matthew is a triple sports star because he takes part in baseball, football, and plays on the basketball team too.

IMPROVING YOUR SENTENCE STRUCTURE

You have learned to avoid monotony and gain variety in style by using simple, compound, and complex sentences. Another way is to combine short, choppy simple sentences into longer and smoother types by means of the following changes:

• Instead of writing a series of short sentences containing ideas of unequal importance, keep the main idea in a main clause and write the supporting information in a helping clause or phrase at the end of the sentence.

Weak	*Better*
The convoy arrived safely. An umbrella of planes helped protect the vessels. Destroyers guarded the ships against attack.	The convoy arrived safely because it was protected against attack by an umbrella of planes and by destroyers.

• Instead of stating an idea in a brief sentence and then tacking on a string of other ideas in loose succession, arrange your information so that you lead up to the main idea by using an introductory clause or phrase.

Weak	*Better*
The pilot had to bail out. There was no more gas in the tank. No landing field was in sight.	Because there was no more gas in the tank and no landing field in sight, the pilot had to bail out.

• Instead of using a series of sentences in disconnected order, keep the main idea intact and change the other sentences into dependent elements, as follows:

1. Combine a series of short sentences into a strong compound sentence.

Weak	*Better*
My sister and I went on a vacation. We went to Boston. We had a wonderful time.	My sister and I went on a vacation to Boston, *and* we had a wonderful time.

2. Change a main clause to a dependent clause.

Weak	*Better*
We couldn't use the car. It needed repair. Jack and I took the bus. Mary and Jane walked.	*Because the car needed repair,* Jack and I took the bus, but Mary and Jane walked.

3. Change a main clause to an appositive phrase.

Weak	*Better*
Jack Brown is my cousin. He is from Chicago. He expects to visit me. It will be during the Christmas vacation.	Jack Brown, *my cousin from Chicago*, expects to visit me during the Christmas vacation.

4. Change a main clause to a prepositional phrase.

Weak	*Better*
I heard that you moved. You moved to Philadelphia. I was surprised.	I was surprised to hear *of your moving to Philadelphia*.

Exercise—Combining Sentences

Combine the short sentences in each group below into one or two smooth, well-constructed sentences. On scrap paper try several ways. Then write your most effective sentence or sentences.

1. I like to play tennis. It is a very exciting game. I play it in the summer. It gives me good exercise.
2. We have some new teachers in our school. There are three of them. Two are women. One is a man.
3. I bought a new book. It is a mystery. It is an exciting story. It is written by a well-known author.
4. Washington is the capital. It is a big city. It also is a beautiful city. My father once took me to Washington. We had a wonderful time.
5. I can't go to the movies. The reason is that I haven't done my homework. I wish I could go.
6. I am going to a concert. It is to take place on Saturday. I am going with a friend. The concert is for charity.

7. People in America are free. They can work and play. People in this country should be glad they are Americans.
8. I like to read books. I have a library. My mother bought me many books. I have a large collection.
9. Russia is a very big country. It is very cold there in the winter. It is especially cold in a region called Siberia. They have a lot of snow in Siberia.
10. Riding a bike at night is dangerous. Many bicyclists are injured. Some are seriously hurt. We must be very careful.

Exercise—Composing Sentences

The following questions are designed to measure your power to think and to express your thoughts correctly. Try to use the three kinds of sentences which you have learned (*simple, compound,* and *complex*) in order to obtain practice in writing a variety of sentences. Occasionally, begin an answer with a different element (*word, phrase, clause*) in order to avoid the deadly monotony of subject, verb, object.

1. What three things can you find out about a word in a dictionary?
2. Why do you like vacations?
3. State at least two reasons why one should be educated.
4. Give an example of the proverb, "A rolling stone gathers no moss."
5. What famous person in the news today do you admire? Why?
6. Name your favorite newspaper and state the section you enjoy most.
7. Why do you (or don't you) like to travel?
8. What is the most important decision you ever made?
9. Define the terms "synonym" and "antonym."
10. What is your hobby and how does it help you in your daily life?
11. Give an example of the proverb, "Make hay while the sun shines."
12. Name three books that you read recently and state which you liked best.
13. Is it better to live in the city or in the country?
14. How would you entertain an out-of-town friend who is visiting you? State his or her name, in what city he or she lives, and the occasion for the visit.
15. What are you most puzzled about?
16. What was your most embarrassing moment?
17. If your pencil could speak, what do you suppose it would say?
18. What famous building, museum, or place of interest have you visited and on what occasion?
19. Tell your friend that you will be unable to keep an engagement. State his or her name, the nature of the appointment, and why you can't keep it.
20. Give an example of the proverb, "A bird in the hand is worth two in the bush."

Chapter 4

Avoiding the Sentence Fragment, Comma Fault, and Run-On Blunder

A. THE SENTENCE FRAGMENT

DEFINITION

A *fragment* is an incomplete statement. It is only a part of a sentence.

Look at the following list of ideas and try to decide whether they are considered good English.

1. Yes!
2. Hello, there!
3. Who?
4. Anybody home?
5. Peddlers not allowed.
6. All deliveries through the basement.
7. Center lane for passing only.
8. Keep under refrigeration.

Of course, *these are all acceptable* because they are intended as parts of statements with other words (italicized below) either previously expressed or understood. They are not careless errors in forming sentences. Match them with these possible situations and you will see why they are all right.

1. (*Are you going to the movies?*) ANSWER: Yes!
   ("I am going to the movies" is understood.)
2. Hello, (*I want to speak with you*) there!
   (This may be just a greeting between neighbors.)
3. Who (*is calling, please*)?
   (A telephone question to find out the name of the caller.)
4. (*Is there*) Anybody home?
   (This may be said by someone knocking at the front door.)
5. Peddlers (*are*) not allowed.
   (This may be a sign at the door of a private home or apartment.)
6. All deliveries (*are to be made*) through the basement.
   (This may be a sign at a school or an apartment or a hotel.)
7. Center lane (*is to be used*) for passing only.
   (Highway traffic sign for motorists gives the regulation.)
8. Keep (*this*) under refrigeration (*or else it may spoil*).
   (A notice to the person using certain food jars; for example, a bottle of ketchup.)

WHEN IS IT WRONG TO USE A FRAGMENT?

A fragment is wrong when it is a careless error written as though it were a complete sentence. It usually occurs in a letter or composition put together hastily or thoughtlessly. You can avoid a fragment by checking all your written work before handing it in for correction. Ask yourself as you reread a sentence:

1. Is it a complete statement? Are any necessary words missing?
2. Does the sentence have a subject and a predicate verb?
3. Can it stand alone to make sense, or should it be connected to another sentence?

Here are some typical fragments to watch for in your written work.

FRAGMENT: Everyone pushing and shoving.
CORRECTED: Everyone was pushing and shoving.

FRAGMENT: Hoping to see you soon.
CORRECTED: I hope to see you soon.

FRAGMENT: On the second floor of the building.
CORRECTED: On the second floor of the building is the nurse's office.

FRAGMENT: While Barbara cleaned the garage.
CORRECTED: While Barbara cleaned the garage, Louis washed the car.

FRAGMENT: I ate quickly. Because I was hungry.
CORRECTED: I ate quickly because I was hungry.

FRAGMENT: When the rain started. We fled for shelter.
CORRECTED: When the rain started, we fled for shelter.

Exercise—Correcting the Sentence Fragment

Rewrite the following fragments into correct and complete sentences.

1. Came home at eight o'clock today.
2. At the restaurant on Main and First Streets.
3. When the repairman came to the house to fix the TV.
4. The girl who lives next door.
5. William and Robert went to the show. Also Mary.
6. Expecting to start work next week.
7. Because the clock stopped.
8. Write the letter in ink. Not pencil.
9. I saw Dick. Who was walking with Ed.
10. As we were walking to school.
11. The soldiers and sailors in the parade.
12. Everyone shouting and screaming. That's because our team won the game.

13. Until he started his speech.
14. Just a few feet beyond the next traffic light.
15. I can't swim. But I should like to learn.

B. THE COMMA FAULT

Whenever you finish writing a sentence, you put a period to mark the end. If you forget the period and use a comma instead, you keep running one sentence right into the next. Thus, you have committed the **comma fault**.

This kind of loose rambling along destroys the unity needed for clear expression of ideas. To remedy this situation, you may do the following.

FOUR WAYS OF CORRECTING THE COMMA FAULT

1. Divide the comma fault into separate sentences.
   FAULTY: Pebbles came barking to greet me, I gave her a bone.
                                                        comma
   Cut into two sentences by using a *period* instead of a comma.
   CORRECT: Pebbles came barking to greet me. I gave her a bone.
                                                        period

2. Make one of the clauses a *subordinate clause* by showing the connection between ideas.
   FAULTY: Dad sliced the turkey, Mother called us in.
                                         comma
   CORRECT: *When* Dad sliced the turkey, Mother called us in.
              Dad sliced the turkey, *after* Mother called us in.

3. Join the main clauses by a *coordinate conjunction* if the ideas have equal importance.
   FAULTY: The car buyers wanted the new models, the prices
                                                          comma
              went up according to the demand.
   CORRECT: The car buyers wanted the new models, *and so* the prices went up according to the demand.

4. Punctuate with a *semicolon* between main clauses, not by a comma. If necessary, insert a conjunction.
   FAULTY: We are born, we live, we die.
   CORRECT: We are born; we live; we die.

C. THE RUN-ON BLUNDER

When two sentences are run together as if they were one, the result is the *run-on blunder*.

FOUR WAYS OF CORRECTING THE RUN-ON BLUNDER

1. Divide the run-on blunder into separate sentences.

   RUN-ON: She left an hour ago she should return soon.

   CORRECT: She left an hour ago. She should return soon.

   period

2. Join the two sentences by inserting a comma plus a coordinate conjunction.

   CORRECT: She left an hour ago, *but* she should return soon.

   comma

3. Subordinate one of the sentences.

   CORRECT: Since she left an hour ago, she should return soon.

4. Punctuate the two sentences with a semicolon.

   CORRECT: She left an hour ago; she should return soon.

   semicolon

Exercise—Correcting the Comma Fault and the Run-On Blunder

Rewrite the following faults into correct sentences. Vary your sentences.

1. We were cold and hungry, we had a hot dinner when we returned home.
2. It is an interesting book you should read it.
3. Mother said to be home at eight don't be late.
4. The door was locked, I was worried, where was everybody?
5. We are going to school you go home.
6. Let's hurry, we are late.
7. Fred is here, he wants to see you.
8. I looked everywhere for my hat I couldn't find it.
9. She bought a new dress it is pretty.
10. The window was open, the rain came in.
11. Please be on time don't be late.
12. We watched the football game it was exciting it was on TV.
13. The child fell, she bruised her knee, she cried.
14. I like to row a boat it is good exercise.
15. We walked to the station we had ample time to meet the train.

Review of Sentence Structure

Review—Subject and Verb

Write the subject in one column and the verb in a second column.

1. About an hour ago Ralph called.
2. Do you want me to help you?
3. Buy a loaf of bread and a bottle of milk.
4. Onto the couch jumped the dog.
5. Olga, Betty, Shirley, and I played tennis.
6. May I go for a walk?
7. In the meantime Jane did her homework.
8. Frequently I walk to school.
9. Have you written to Aunt Sally?
10. Jill and Judy, my twin sisters, enter college this fall.

Review—Kinds of Sentences

Change these imperative sentences into either declarative or interrogative sentences. Punctuate properly! The following models are provided as answers to sentence 1.

DECLARATIVE: You should shake this bottle well before using.
INTERROGATIVE: Will you shake this bottle well before using?

1. Shake this bottle well before using.
2. Please turn off the lights when leaving the room.
3. Be sure to put your coat on if you go outdoors.
4. Answer all the questions to get full credit.
5. Keep your wallet in a safe place to avoid losing it.
6. Feed the fish regularly at the same time every day.
7. Take a two-mile walk just to keep trim.
8. Drink a glass of milk with every meal for health's sake.
9. Save your money now, and you will have it later on.
10. Don't mix pickles and ice cream.

Review—Compound and Complex Sentences

Classify the following sentences as *compound* (CD) or *complex* (CX). Identify the conjunction, subordinate or coordinate, as the case may be.

1. New York and Los Angeles are capital cities, and both have large populations.
2. The gardener planted trees which provided shade in the summer and blossoms in spring.
3. Does the Federal Government guarantee the safety of the money that you deposit in a local savings bank?
4. If winter comes, can spring be far behind?
5. Does the gambler enjoy being with people, or does he want to win?
6. Whenever I hear church bells at night, I feel the comforting reminder of living in the city, not the wilderness.
7. Texas is a very large state, but Alaska is even larger.
8. Since teenagers have shown such interest in buying records, manufacturers have produced many albums of popular songs.
9. Frank was twenty pounds overweight until he started to diet.
10. "Shall I pick you up at the dentist's office this afternoon, or will you take the bus home?" Larry asked.

Review—Sentence Faults

In one or two sentences each, rewrite these faulty word groups.

1. The water boiled. I put in a tea bag. I made a cup of tea.
2. Entering the house, the clock struck twelve.
3. My favorite sports are hiking, swimming, and an occasional game of golf.
4. Without my glasses just when the lights went out during the storm.
5. I can't go with you, my parents want me to get home early.
6. We'll meet at Disney World we'll have a good time together.
7. They spread salt. The salt melted the ice. The streets became clear.
8. To lose weight, Albert gave up candy, ice cream, and all kinds of goodies made with flour, butter, and sugar.
9. Our school newspaper with front-page stories and letters to the editor and sports articles.
10. Washington High had already won three games, and our team had lost three and as you know we beat them in the last five seconds of the game.
11. After every meal brushing your teeth and gums vigorously to remove food particles.
12. "Good-bye, Henry," I said, that's the last time I saw him.
13. Tell Fred not to call me I won't be home tonight.

14. A gong sounded. It was a fire drill. The pupils marched out.
15. At last I found a beautiful watch to tell time with luminous hands.
16. Careers that require training, study, and experience for high salaries and promotion.
17. The best way to study is by concentrating on a problem there should be no distractions.
18. He fell down. His head hit the ground. He looked hurt.
19. Susan B. Anthony wanted to get women the right to vote in America so she started the women's suffrage movement and she was elected to the American Hall of Fame.
20. Our country has built several nuclear plants. Because nuclear power can supplement coal, oil, and other fuels.

Review—Sentence Sense

Sentence sense shows that you know how to divide groups of words properly according to their meaning. Rewrite the following passage by dividing it into complete and appropriate sentences. Be sure to use the correct punctuation and capitalization.

WHAT IS A TEENAGER?

Between the innocence of babyhood and the dignity of adulthood we find a mysterious creature called a teenager teenagers come in assorted sizes weights and colors but they all have one thing in common they live every second of every minute of every day as if it were their last day on earth

Teenagers can be found gathering everywhere the corner soda fountain the record shop and in the middle of the street you can usually hear them before you see them they have the energy of a pocket-sized atom bomb the curiosity of a cat the lungs of a dictator and the imagination of a Jules Verne

The teenager is a composite of many wonderful and terrifying things the female of the species is a combination of Eve Salome and Florence Nightingale she likes clothes dancing and the boy next-door the male is slightly different he likes the woods hunting fishing and although he likes girls he may show the shyness of a violet when meeting one who else can make a proud parent miserable delighted and embarrassed at the same time

In spite of everything the teenager is a magical creature with a bottle of cola in one hand and the future of the world in the other

PART THREE

Learn the Basic Rules

What is *grammar?*

Grammar is the logic of language. For example, to make good sense there must be agreement in number between subject and verb: "A fool and his money *are* soon parted." The verb must be plural to agree with the plural subject *fool* and *money*.

What is *correct usage?*

Correct usage means using the right word to fit the meaning. For example, you may not say, "She *learned* me how to use the typewriter." Correct usage requires *taught*. "He borrowed a dollar *off* me" should be "He borrowed a dollar *from* me." These errors deal with certain parts of speech: the verb and the preposition. All told, there are eight parts of speech. Learn to recognize them as part of the basic rules of language.

Chapter 5

The Parts of Speech

WHY DO WE NEED TO KNOW THE PARTS OF SPEECH?

Every activity has its own special language. We need to learn the way to communicate with each other whenever we talk about sports, cooking, or making money. For example, can you talk intelligently about basketball without using expressions such as *lay up, rebound, foul shot, zone defense, freeze,* etc.? Can you cook without understanding such directions as *deep-fry, simmer, knead dough, cream shortening, sift flour,* etc.? Can you manage money without knowing the meaning of *salary, bonus, dividends, interest income, risk capital,* etc.?

Just as we must learn these special vocabularies, we need to learn the parts of speech in order to know what the elements are that we put together in making acceptable sentences. For example, when your teacher asks you to use a conjunction to connect a dependent clause to the rest of the sentence, do you know what to do? To improve your writing skill, you need to know as much about the grammar of our language as a good cook knows about recipes and an athlete knows about sports. Let's try it!

DEFINITION

Parts of speech **are the labels telling how words are used in a sentence.** There are eight parts of speech: *noun, pronoun, verb, adjective, adverb, preposition, conjunction, interjection.*

QUICK QUIZ

Can you match these definitions with the right parts of speech?

DEFINITIONS	PARTS OF SPEECH
1. expresses action or state of being	*a.* noun
2. connects a phrase to another word	*b.* pronoun
3. a substitute for a noun	*c.* verb
4. connects a clause to the rest of the sentence	*d.* adverb
5. a name-word showing the doer or receiver of an action	*e.* adjective
6. describes a verb, an adjective, or an adverb	*f.* interjection
7. shows strong emotion	*g.* preposition
8. describes a noun	*h.* conjunction

Answers: 1-*c*, 2-*g*, 3-*b*, 4-*h*, 5-*a*, 6-*d*, 7-*f*, 8-*e*

HOW CAN YOU TELL WHAT PART OF SPEECH A WORD IS?

A word is labeled as a certain part of speech according to the way it is used in its sentence. Thus, the same word may be a noun in one sentence and a verb in another.

water used as a ***noun:***	Drink *water* with your meals.
water used as a **verb:**	Please *water* the flowers.
water used as an ***adjective:***	Do you like *water* sports?

Here are other examples of the same word (*down*) used as different parts of speech:

The temperature went <u>down</u>.
adverb

The ship sailed <u>down</u> the river.
preposition

The football team made a first <u>down</u>.
noun

The truck gained speed on the <u>down</u> grade.
adjective

The wrestler <u>downed</u> his opponent three times.
verb

From a study of *down* in the sentences above, you realize that before you can classify any word as a particular part of speech you must determine how it is used.

When you refer to the dictionary as part of your training in vocabulary building, you will notice that the various meanings for words are grouped according to their parts of speech. These are indicated by abbreviations:

n.	noun	*adj.*	adjective
pron.	pronoun	*prep.*	preposition
v.	verb	*conj.*	conjunction
adv.	adverb	*interj.*	interjection

THE EIGHT PARTS OF SPEECH

A *noun* is a word used as the name of something; it may be a person, a place, a thing, or a quality.

PERSONS:	boy, woman, friend
PLACES:	home, school, park
THINGS:	school, pencil, book
QUALITIES:	truth, honesty, love

A *pronoun* is a word used instead of a noun; it is a substitute for the name of a person, place, or thing.

I, you, he, she, it, who, etc.
me, him, her, us, them, whom, etc.
my, mine, your, yours, hers, our, etc.

A *verb* is a word used to describe an action or to state a condition.

sing, play, go, work, study, is, are, am

An *adjective* is a word used to describe or limit a noun; it modifies the meaning of the noun. It tells *what kind? how much? how many?*

> DESCRIBING ADJECTIVES: tall, short, broad, fast, exciting
> LIMITING ADJECTIVES: six, few, many, some, fifty

The words *a*, *an*, and *the* are adjectives that are also called *articles.*

An *adverb* is a word that modifies a verb, an adjective, or another adverb. It tells *how? when? where?* etc. (The adverbs are italicized; the modified words are underlined.)

> MODIFYING A VERB: The boy threw the ball *quickly.*
>
> MODIFYING AN ADJECTIVE: Jeanne is an *exceptionally* bright girl.
>
> MODIFYING AN ADVERB: The boy threw the ball *very* quickly.

A *preposition* is a word that introduces a prepositional phrase. (A phrase is a group of words lacking both a subject and a verb.)

> *in* the house, *to* the store, *by* the road, *before* the game

A *conjunction* is a word that connects two or more words, phrases, or clauses.

> and, or, but, since, because, that, if, unless

> WORDS: I like vanilla, strawberry, *and* chocolate ice cream.
>
> PHRASES: You can have more pocket money by earning more *or* by spending less.
>
> CLAUSES: Music appeals to the listener *because* it stirs the emotions.

An *interjection* is a word used to express a sudden or strong emotion.

> alas, hurrah, oh, ah, ouch! wow!

ILLUSTRATION OF THE PARTS OF SPEECH

Each word in the sentences in the box on the next page is classified according to its part of speech. The numbers below the words correspond with the parts of speech listed below the box.

Using the definitions of the eight parts of speech, tell how each word is used in the sentence. For example, *Saturday* is a noun because it is the name of a day of the week; and, according to the definition, a word used as the name of something is a noun.

On Saturday my father gladly took Bertha and me to the game.
  1   2   3   4   5   6   7   8   9 10 11   12

Oh, it was some game! In the ninth inning, Ace Miller hit a homerun
 13 14 15   16   17   18 19   20   21   22   23   24 25   26

and won the game for us. This victory practically assures our team
 27   28   29   30   31 32   33   34   35   36   37   38

of the championship.
 39 40   41

ANSWERS:

1. preposition
2. noun
3. pronoun
4. noun
5. adverb
6. verb
7. noun
8. conjunction
9. pronoun
10. preposition
11. adjective
12. noun
13. interjection
14. pronoun
15. verb
16. adjective
17. noun
18. preposition
19. adjective
20. adjective
21. noun
22. noun
23. noun
24. verb
25. adjective
26. noun
27. conjunction
28. verb
29. adjective
30. noun
31. preposition
32. pronoun
33. adjective
34. noun
35. adverb
36. verb
37. pronoun
38. noun
39. preposition
40. adjective
41. noun

Exercises—Parts of Speech

A. Label each italicized word correctly, by writing the abbreviations:
n., *v.*, *pron.*, *adj.*, *adv.*, *prep.*, *conj.*, or *interj.*

1. Lincoln was an *honest* man.
2. The *girl* did her work well.
3. To *whom* are you talking?
4. I *quickly* went home.
5. There were *four* occupants in the car.
6. We must always have *courage*.
7. My sister came home *late*.
8. It was given *to* the principal.
9. *Always* speak distinctly.
10. Our job *sounds* more interesting.

11. We were *late* to school.
12. That pen is *hers.*
13. He always eats *hurriedly.*
14. The house on the *hill* is old.
15. *In* the ice box is a bottle of milk.
16. Baseball *and* football are exciting sports.
17. We had a *wonderful* time at the circus.
18. That girl sings *very* well.
19. *Say,* what time is it?
20. *Blue* mixed with yellow makes green.

B. Write the part of speech of each italicized word.

1. My brother is a *fine* athlete.
2. We were quietly listening *to* the radio.
3. *Hers* is broken.
4. We carefully *lifted* the package.
5. To *whom* did you address the letter?
6. The cries *rang* through the night.
7. The papers were scattered *by* the wind.
8. The *woman* was elected to Congress.
9. *Sometimes* I help my father.
10. To succeed in life, we must be *ambitious.*
11. Both John *and* Mary are at home.
12. The *late* arrivals had nothing to eat.
13. *Oh,* what a party it was.
14. *Into* the pool dived the dolphins.
15. We played an *interesting* game of checkers.
16. When he gets angry, he sees *red.*
17. There were *seven* players on the field.
18. It *was* an unusually cold morning.
19. Don't lose your *confidence.*
20. The train arrived *early.*

C. Write the part of speech of each italicized word.

1. The timekeeper *clocks* the runners in each race.
2. Grandfather *clocks* are now high-priced antiques.
3. *Alas!* Those days are gone forever.
4. Universities have been faced with *higher* costs per student.
5. To lose weight you must exercise *regularly* and diet sensibly.
6. An obedient youngster behaves *as* he or she is told by adults.
7. She dropped the grains of food *into* the fishbowl.
8. The president of the class is the one *who* deserves most credit.
9. The traffic officer ordered the driver to slow *down.*
10. In the darkness, Gale stumbled *down* the winding staircase.

11. At the precinct, the desk sergeant tried to *book* the prisoner.
12. The judge referred to the *book* of laws before passing sentence.
13. "*Bah!* Humbug!" was Scrooge's opinion of the Christmas spirit.
14. We bent down to help the little girl and picked her up *tenderly*.
15. A bouquet of flowers smells *fresh* when picked in the garden.
16. The hands of the clock *move* slowly when you stare at them.
17. The herd was kept on the *move* by the cowboys.
18. His composition is longer than *mine*.
19. The city is building an office tower *up* the street.
20. The pupils were trained to stand *up* when reciting.

D. Select all the words that illustrate the part of speech mentioned.

1. *nouns:*
   Every person, young or old, has the opportunity to acquire an education.

2. *verbs:*
   We saw the girls in a car ride into town.

3. *pronouns:*
   I called my father and asked him to pick me up at the dentist.

4. *adjectives:*
   He is a strict teacher, and even the lazy students do their English homework.

5. *adverbs:*
   We were always cautioned against crossing the streets slowly or carelessly.

6. *prepositions:*
   From our window we could see the light across the street.

7. *conjunctions:*
   Cookies and milk were served, but neither Kurt nor Marian would eat.

8. *interjections:*
   Oh, what's the use? Well! I like your courage.

Chapter 6

Nouns

Nouns **are name-words used to identify persons, places, things, ideas, animals, qualities.** Everything that exists has a particular name. The word used to label each thing is called a *noun* (from Latin *nomen*, meaning "name").

COMMON AND PROPER NOUNS

Nouns can be divided into two main groups: common nouns and proper nouns.

A *common noun* **is a word used to label any general class of persons, places, or things:** student, friend, city, river, book, flag.

A *proper noun* **is a word used to label a special or particular member of a class of persons, places, or things.**

Spelling gives a clue, too. The common nouns are spelled with *small* letters; the proper nouns always begin with *capital* (large) letters.

COMMON NOUNS	PROPER NOUNS
artist	Michelangelo
student	Helen Smith
poet	Amy Lowell
general	General Robert E. Lee
book	the Bible
building	the White House
day	Sunday
newspaper	the *New York Times*
whale	Moby Dick
city	Venice
institution	Harvard University

Exercise—Proper Nouns

A. Compose five sentences using proper nouns, selecting them from the list above.

B. Capitalize the proper nouns in each sentence.

1. lindberg's plane, the *spirit of st. louis*, is in the smithsonian institution located in washington, d.c.
2. The eiffel tower may be seen in paris, france.
3. The united nations is housed in a building that faces the east river in new york city.
4. In san francisco we dined at joe di maggio's restaurant on the famous fisherman's wharf.
5. The battleship *arizona* is part of a national monument in pearl harbor.

Exercises—Nouns

List the nouns in the following passages, *A* and *B*.

A. Accidents can happen anywhere: a stairway, a bathtub, a crack in the pavement, an icy street, a slippery floor, a scatter rug, a moving vehicle, a pot that boils over, a misstep on a ladder. The list of possibilities is endless.

B. Advertisement: Would you like to know how to win happiness, luck, success? Would you like to find out secrets relating to health, money, work, and friendship? Do you seek fame and fortune? Do you know why some persons stay in a rut while others win their heart's desire? If you want good advice at moderate cost, fill out the enclosed card today!

C. Write the name-word that identifies each thing described below. Check yourself with the scrambled answers at the end of the exercise.

1. an instrument for measuring temperature
2. an outdoor broiler for hamburgers, etc.
3. a flexible rubber or plastic pipe for watering lawns
4. whirling blades for circulating air
5. *on* and *off* mechanism for controlling electric light or power
6. scissorlike tool for cutting wire, turning nuts, etc.
7. pockt-size computer for arithmetic problems
8. a means of rising or climbing
9. closet for storing clothes
10. couch or divan in the living room

> SCRAMBLED ANSWERS: pliers, ladder, hose, switch, sofa, thermometer, grill, wardrobe, calculator, fan.

D. Add appropriate nouns to complete these statements.

1. Trees and __?__ bloom in the spring.
2. Airplanes carrying __?__ and __?__ go from city to city.
3. Unexpected laughter after __?__ makes us happy.
4. Tables with __?__ make dining more pleasant.
5. The talented __?__ and __?__ at the school show won our applause.
6. Knives, __?__, and __?__ made of silver are brought out for company.
7. Making the bed properly for sleeping requires sheets, __?__, and __?__.
8. The basic tools to carry in the trunk of a car include __?__, __?__, and __?__.
9. The two great commandments are these: "Love your __?__ and love your __?__."
10. Radio programs consist chiefly of __?__, __?__, and __?__.

HOW ARE NOUNS USED IN SENTENCES?

The noun is the doer or the receiver of an action. As a principal part of a sentence, the noun is usually found as the subject of the verb or as the object of the verb. You can identify the noun by looking for the person or thing spoken about. Sometimes you will find the noun used as the object of a preposition. In every instance, the noun is a name-word used to label a person, place, or thing.

1. Noun used as subject of the verb:

Your *sandwich* is ready.
     S   V

Our scout *patrol* hiked through the woods.
          S   V

The steering *wheel* turned to the right.
          S   V

My *grandmother* gave me a book.
     S   V

2. Noun used as direct object of the verb:

The comedian's jokes amused the *listeners*.
             V   D.O.

The blizzard blocked the mountain *pass*.
         V   D.O.

A cut in taxes pleases the average *citizen*.
         V   D.O.

Our school bought a new trophy *case*.
        V   D.O.

3. Noun used as object of a preposition:

The love of *country* is called patriotism.
P   O.P.

Working for a *living* helps you mature.
P   O.P.

Sugar in *soda* makes it taste sweet.
P O.P.

The patient relaxed after the *injection*.
P   O.P.

Exercise—Nouns Used in Sentences

List the nouns in each sentence. Opposite each noun, write one of these abbreviations to tell how the noun is used:

S. = noun used as subject of the verb
D.O. = noun used as direct object of the verb
O.P. = noun used as object of a preposition

1. Mary Ann put her hair in curlers.
2. My son shined his shoes before school.
3. A good child does some chores around the house.
4. Our neighbor parked his car in the driveway.
5. The telephone rang twice and stopped without reason.
6. The sound of music lulled the patient.
7. Alice bought two quarts of milk at the supermarket.
8. Mother waxed the floor with a machine.
9. The team lost the game by two points.
10. During the emergency, the snowplows cleared the streets.
11. Many flowers will bloom for twelve months with proper care.
12. Louise cooked the beefburgers in the backyard.
13. Matilda tossed the ball into the basket.
14. Under different lights, flowers grow stronger or weaker.
15. Industrial wastes have polluted the streams near cities.
16. Eva brushed her hair into a smooth wave.
17. Ramón has always wanted a house in the country.
18. The caddy found the ball under the hedge.
19. A cardinal fought with a jay over the crumbs.
20. Before the rain, Joe washed and polished the car.

ENDINGS OF COMMON NOUNS

You will recognize many nouns by certain endings. Study these endings and at the same time increase your vocabulary through a better knowledge of how words are formed.

1. Endings showing an *agent* or *doer:*

er	speaker, player, voter
or	actor, supervisor, creditor
ee	trustee, employee, payee
ive	captive, fugitive, native
ist	dentist, scientist, organist

2. Endings describing a *condition, state,* or *action:*

ship	friendship, worship, hardship
dom	freedom, wisdom, kingdom
ing	swimming, learning, writing
ness	kindness, holiness, goodness
hood	childhood, neighborhood, womanhood
acy	privacy, diplomacy, democracy
ance	elegance, disturbance, repentance
ence	patience, absence, innocence

3. Endings naming an *idea, quality,* or *general notion:*

ity	equality, fraternity, maturity
ation	admiration, conversation, imagination
ment	government, temperament, establishment
ology	biology, zoology, geology
ism	patriotism, magnetism, criticism
ure	creature, literature, measure
ute	tribute, institute, salute

Exercise—Endings of Nouns

Using your dictionary to help you, add another example for each ending below.

ery	machinery, treachery		*ant*	servant, merchant
ude	altitude, longitude		*ent*	incident, rodent
sion	mansion, confusion		*ice*	practice, justice
mony	ceremony, testimony		*age*	village, cottage
nym	homonym, antonym			

PLURAL OF NOUNS

The regular way of spelling the plural of nouns is by adding an *s* to the singular. There are some nouns which require an *es,* and a few which change a letter or letters. The following guidelines will help you to form the plural of nouns.

Add *s* to singular nouns, provided the *s* does not thereby add another syllable.

Singular	*Plural*	*Singular*	*Plural*
boy	boys	girl	girls

Add *s* to singular nouns ending in *o* preceded by a vowel (*a, e, i, o, u*).

Singular	*Plural*	*Singular*	*Plural*
stereo	stereos	radio	radios

Add *s* to singular nouns ending in *y* preceded by a vowel.

Singular	*Plural*	*Singular*	*Plural*
valley	valleys	monkey	monkeys

Add *s* to the first word of singular hyphenated nouns.

Singular	*Plural*	*Singular*	*Plural*
son-in-law	sons-in-law	commander-in-chief	commanders-in-chief

Add *es* to singular nouns ending in *s, sh, ch, x,* or *z.*

Singular	*Plural*	*Singular*	*Plural*
miss	misses	bench	benches
wish	wishes	box	boxes
waltz	waltzes		

Add *es* to singular nouns ending in *o* preceded by a consonant (*b, c, d, f, g,* etc.).

Singular	*Plural*	*Singular*	*Plural*
hero	heroes	potato	potatoes

Add *es* to nouns ending in *y* preceded by a consonant, changing *y* to *i.*

Singular	*Plural*	*Singular*	*Plural*
lady	ladies	sky	skies

Some nouns ending in *f* or *fe* form their plural by changing the *f* or *fe* to v and adding *es.*

Singular	Plural	Singular	Plural
calf	calves	knife	knives
life	lives	wife	wives

Some nouns form their plural by a change of form.

Singular	Plural	Singular	Plural
foot	feet	mouse	mice
tooth	teeth	louse	lice
goose	geese	child	children

Some nouns keep the same spelling for the plural as for the singular.

Singular	Plural	Singular	Plural
deer	deer	sheep	sheep

Some nouns form their plural by changing *man* to *men*, and *woman* to *women.*

Singular	Plural	Singular	Plural
motorman	motormen	statesman	statesmen
saleswoman	saleswomen	Congresswoman	Congresswomen

All nouns ending in *ful* add *s* at the end to form the plural.

Singular	Plural	Singular	Plural
teaspoonful	teaspoonfuls	handful	handfuls

Some nouns are always plural in form:

news	pliers	series
tidings	eyeglasses	civics
scissors	clothes	politics
pants	suds	species
trousers	thanks	mathematics

Remember this: When in doubt, check with the dictionary!

Exercises—Plural of Nouns

A. Write the plural form of each of the following nouns.

1. calf	21. mouse	41. life
2. knife	22. bush	42. country
3. piano	23. lady	43. loaf
4. ax	24. valley	44. leaf
5. deer	25. child	45. spoonful
6. sky	26. salesman	46. friend
7. potato	27. fox	47. foot
8. army	28. radio	48. half
9. city	29. cupful	49. pocketful
10. lily	30. duty	50. reply
11. tooth	31. mother-in-law	51. copy
12. inch	32. wharf	52. enemy
13. fly	33. guest	53. son-in-law
14. stereo	34. tomato	54. pailful
15. goose	35. sheep	55. play
16. mouthful	36. pony	56. grocery
17. journey	37. woman	57. attorney
18. mosquito	38. thief	58. story
19. baby	39. tax	59. shelf
20. wife	40. louse	60. candy

B. Rewrite each of the following sentences, changing the singular subject to the plural and making other changes necessary to make the new sentence correct.

1. In the next room the child is playing.
2. The younger man has been selected for the team.
3. Is the woman running the election campaign?
4. My tooth was examined by a dentist.
5. The visitor has gone to the baseball game.
6. A leaf has fallen from the tree.
7. May the boy go to the movies tonight?
8. The mouse has eaten the cheese.
9. This fly is annoying me.
10. My sister-in-law visited us.
11. The box was delivered by truck this morning.
12. A baby needs much loving care.
13. My brother-in-law works for a bank.
14. The pencil is on my desk.
15. At the ceremony, the hero was given a silver medal.

FORMING THE POSSESSIVE OF NOUNS

The *possessive case* shows ownership. The use of an apostrophe and the letter *s* at the end of a noun shows that something belongs to that noun. For example, "the captain's quarters" refers to the room belonging to the captain aboard a ship.

Here are some illustrative sentences using possessive nouns.

> The girl's sculpture is beautiful.
> Here is Fred's pencil.
> The men's uniforms are brand new.

If the last letter of a noun is an *s*, you need to add only the apostrophe to make it possessive. You do not add an extra *s*. Notice these examples:

> She makes ladies' hats.
> The princesses' dresses looked stunning.
> The monkeys' antics were amusing.
> All the players' lockers had a gold star.

However, when a proper noun ends in *s*, you may use either *s'* or *s's*.

> Dickens' novel or Dickens's novel
> Frances' coat or Frances's coat
> Lois' book or Lois's book
> Hughes' house or Hughes's house

The preferred usage, however, is to add just the apostrophe and no *s*.

• Rule I. Possessive Singular

To form the possessive of a singular noun, you add an apostrophe and the letter *s*.

> skater   + apostrophe and letter *s* = skater's partner
> cousin   + apostrophe and letter *s* = cousin's house
> neighbor + apostrophe and letter *s* = neighbor's fence

• Rule II. Possessive Plural

To form the possessive of a plural noun, make sure that you first write the correct form of the plural. Then, if the plural ends in the letter *s*, you add just an apostrophe. (You do not add an extra *s*.)

> There was a sale on ladies' coats.
> The girls' spelling team beat the boys' team.
> Our parents' dues were paid to the P.T.A.

But if the plural does not end in the letter *s*, you add an apostrophe and *s* to form the possessive.

> The men's group meets every Friday night.
> My mother belongs to the women's bridge club.
> The scout followed the children's path in the woods.

Notice the difference in meaning for each pair below.

1. *a.* The girl's jokes made him laugh. (only one girl)
   b. The girls' jokes made him laugh. (two or more girls)

2. *a.* The boy's skates were stolen. (only one boy)
   b. The boys' skates were stolen. (two or more boys)

Exercises—Possessive Case of Nouns

A. Following the models given below, write the missing words on your answer paper. Be sure to notice the headings as a guide to whether you are to supply the singular noun or the plural noun, and the possessive forms.

SINGULAR NOUN	POSSESSIVE SINGULAR	PLURAL NOUN	POSSESSIVE PLURAL
woman	woman's	women	women's
Jones	Jones'	Joneses	Joneses'
brother-in-law	brother-in-law's	brothers-in-law	brothers-in-law's
1. hunter	____	hunters	____
2. ____	parent's	parents	____
3. friend	____	____	friends'
4. ____	____	pigeons	____
5. storekeeper	____	____	____
6. ____	secretary's	____	____
7. ____	____	owners	____
8. ____	____	____	players'
9. druggist	____	____	____
10. ____	plumber's	____	____
11. ____	____	coaches	____
12. ____	____	____	runners'
13. sister-in-law	____	____	____
14. ____	aunt's	____	____
15. ____	____	uncles	____
16. lady	____	____	____
17. ____	____	____	authors'
18. teacher	____	____	____
19. ____	____	Smiths	____
20. child	____	____	____

B. Write the correct form of the possessive singular or possessive plural as required in each example below. Review Rules I and II, on pages 53–54.

1. Websters Dictionary
2. The secretarys desk
3. Shakespeares plays
4. The womans reply
5. The A & Ps prices
6. Americas first president
7. Englands Prime Minister
8. Sicilys latest flood
9. The ladies garments
10. The mens shop

AGREEMENT OF SUBJECT NOUN WITH VERB

You already know that a noun may be singular or plural, depending on whether it refers to one person, place, or thing—or whether it refers to more than one. Naturally, the verb used with the noun must agree with the noun. Can you choose the correct verbs to match the nouns in the following sentences?

1. Some students (are, is) sitting in the wrong seats.
2. Here (come, comes) Mary and Louis to join us.
3. Neither John nor his friends (is, are) going to the game.
4. Good news (is, are) not often broadcast over the radio.
5. Mathematics (are, is) my most difficult subject.
6. Barbara with all her playmates (is, are) in the backyard.
7. Our state, not the cities, (pay, pays) all welfare expenses.
8. The leader of the musicians (decide, decides) what to play.
9. Panama, not the United States, (control, controls) the Canal.
10. The cat and the canary (watch, watches) every move they make.

Answers:

1. are
2. come
3. are
4. is
5. is
6. is
7. pays
8. decides
9. controls
10. watch

If you got 100% correct, congratulations to you! If you did not get them all right, you must pay attention to the rules explained below.

- **Rule I.** Subject nouns connected by *and* require a plural verb.

    CORRECT: The <u>hours and minutes</u> *divide* the day into sleeping, work-

    compound subject   pl.

    ing, and playing time.

    CORRECT: <u>Boys and girls</u> together *make* coeducation pleasant.

    compound subject   pl.

- **Rule II.** **Introductory expressions such as** *There is, There are, Here is, Here are* must agree with the subject noun or nouns that follow.

> CORRECT: There *is* a *visitor* at the door.
> sing.   sing.

> CORRECT: There *are sugar and milk* on the table.
> pl.   compound subject

> CORRECT: Here *is* the *fish* that I caught.
> sing.   sing.

> CORRECT: Here *are* the *books* that I have read.
> pl.   pl.

> CORRECT: Here *come* my *father and mother.*
> pl.   compound subject

- **Rule III.** After *either . . . or, neither . . . nor,* the verb must agree with whichever noun stands nearer to the verb.

> CORRECT: Either John or Mary *is* at home.
> CORRECT: Either the girl or the boys *are* to blame.
> CORRECT: Neither her sisters nor Helen *is* so tall as Ruth.
> CORRECT: Neither the teacher nor the pupils *are* in the room.

- **Rule IV.** Certain nouns ending in the letter *s* look as though they are plural, but they are considered singular because they either express a single idea or represent a single sum. Examples: *news, series, politics, civics, mathematics, physics; ten dollars, four tons,* etc.

> CORRECT: There *is* good *news* today.
> sing.

> CORRECT: *Five dollars* a week *is* my allowance.
> sing.

- **Rule V.** A noun followed by a phrase sometimes causes confusion as to whether the verb agrees with the subject noun or the noun in the phrase which comes between.

> CORRECT: The *boys* in the front row *are* a bit noisy.
> subj.   phrase   V

> (The noun *boys* is the subject; the phrase *in the front row* stands between the subject and verb.)

> CORRECT: The *soldier* in the ranks *salutes* the general.
> subj.   phrase   V

> (The noun *soldier* is the subject; the phrase *in the ranks* stands between the subject and verb.)

Exercises—Agreement of Subject Noun With Verb

A. In each of the following sentences, write the word in parentheses that makes the correct agreement of subject noun with verb.

1. A boy and his dog (makes, make) inseparable companions.
2. There (is, are) a state in the United States larger than Texas.
3. The commuters on the bus (stand, stands) when it is crowded.
4. Barbara says physics (is, are) easier than chemistry.
5. The fingers and toes (add, adds) up to twenty digits.
6. Neither Mary nor Lisa (is, are) so athletic as Ruth.
7. Politics as a career (offers, offer) an exciting way of life.
8. Over two hundred separate bones (makes, make) up your body.
9. Checkers, chess, and reading (is, are) favorite rainy-day pastimes.
10. There (was, were) bread and butter and jam on the table for us.
11. Neither Rafael nor Ernesto (owns, own) a transistor radio.
12. Fifty dollars for a dress (are, is) too much to pay.
13. The winner of the first three races (get, gets) a gold medal.
14. Neither Alice nor her sisters (speaks, speak) French well.
15. There (is, are) three parts to memorize in this play.

B. In each of the following sentences, write the word in parentheses that makes the correct agreement of subject noun with verb.

1. During the summer, Frank and Jack (work, works) as waiters in a hotel.
2. The package of books (have, has) been mislaid.
3. Neither Ben nor Max (play, plays) the piano satisfactorily.
4. There (is, are) days when I cannot concentrate on homework.
5. Our silo is filled because five tons of hay (is, are) stored in it.
6. The bouquet of roses (has, have) been placed in the jar.
7. Spring and summer (are, is) my favorite seasons for outdoor recreation.
8. Either Laura or Agnes or Deborah (were, was) to blame for it.
9. Here (is, are) the store where I bought my shoes.
10. TV news (are, is) more dramatic than radio newscasts.
11. Another box of apples (were, was) received by express.
12. I find that math and science (require, requires) more study time.
13. Neither the coach nor the players (is, are) to be blamed for the poor showing of the team.
14. The owner of the apartments (allows, allow) no pets in the building.
15. Mother said there (are, is) chores to be done this afternoon.

Review of Nouns

A. Supply the information required to complete the statements below.

1. A noun is a name-word used to identify a __?__, __?__, or __?__.
2. Two kinds of nouns we have studied are called __?__ nouns (used to label a general class of things) and __?__ nouns (used to label a particular member of a class of things).
3. Spelling provides a clue to the kind of noun because __?__ nouns are spelled with small letters, but __?__ nouns are capitalized.
4. Nouns may be used in sentences to show the doer or the receiver of an action. Thus, a noun may be used as the __?__ of the verb, or as the __?__ of the verb, or as the object of a __?__.

B. Nouns may be formed by certain endings. Give three examples of nouns formed by each of these endings:

1. *er*	5. *ment*	8. *sion*
2. *ist*	6. *ation*	9. *ship*
3. *ance*	7. *ism*	10. *nym*
4. *ity*		

C. Plurals of most nouns are formed by adding __?__ or __?__ to the singular noun. Form the correct plural for each of these nouns.

1. church	5. player	8. tenement
2. hero	6. box	9. sister-in-law
3. valley	7. miss	10. editor-in-chief
4. radio		

D. Give the correct spelling (with apostrophe and letter *s* where necessary) to show the possessive singular and the possessive plural for each noun listed below.

1. boy	3. man	5. lady	7. parent	9. student
2. girl	4. woman	6. neighbor	8. Smith	10. turkey

E. Write the form of the verb that makes the correct agreement of noun with verb.

1. There (was, were) a girl and her mother ahead of us.
2. Either the shoppers or the checker (were, was) in a hurry.
3. Here (stand, stands) the rock the Pilgrims landed on.
4. Neither the players nor the coach (have, has) the right score.
5. Women and children (go, goes) first in leaving a sinking ship.

6. The crate of oranges (were, was) shipped to us C.O.D.
7. The riders on the bus (was, were) making loud noises.
8. The drawers in the desk (are, is) full of papers.
9. The pictures in the window (is, are) those of houses for sale.
10. Either Tom or his brothers (are, is) responsible for losing the key.

F. Write each noun and label it according to the way it is used in the sentence.

S.   subject of verb
D.O.   direct object of verb
O.P.   object of preposition

1. The painting on the wall belongs to my cousin.
2. The sun shines directly on the plants in my window.
3. Loans from banks must be repaid with interest.
4. After the game, the winner shook hands with the loser.
5. Our breakfast begins our day with lively chatter.
6. The briefcase of the lawyer was found in the street.
7. Our friends' parents hired a taxi for the evening.
8. Barbara met Ginger at the museum yesterday.
9. The students' committee recommended another dance.
10. The proceeds of the event went to a worthwhile charity.

G. Write the nouns in these humorous statements.

1. People are funny. They want the front of the bus, the back of the church, and the middle of the road.
2. If you do not wear seat belts, be sure to wear a soft felt hat to protect your ears as your head goes through the windshield.
3. Many hands make light work, but too many cooks spoil the broth.

Chapter 7

Pronouns

Pronouns **are words used in place of nouns.**

You recall that a noun is a name-word used to label a person, place, or thing. Now, a pronoun is a word used in place of the name-word. The reason that we use a pronoun is to avoid repeating the same noun in a sentence.

John told *John's* father that *John* was hungry.
          noun   noun

John told *his* father that *he* was hungry.
          pronoun   pronoun

A. PERSONAL PRONOUNS

The pronouns are a small group of words, but they are very useful in everyday speaking and writing because they refer to the many thousands of words found in our language. You recognize them easily because they serve as shortcuts in practically every sentence. For example, in the two sentences you have just read, you probably noticed the pronouns used: *they, our, you,* and *them.* These are called *personal pronouns*—the most important kind of pronoun.

PERSON AND NUMBER

Personal pronouns **stand for persons, except** *it* **which stands for things.** Personal pronouns are often the cause of errors because they change form according to whether they stand for one or more

> *persons speaking,*
> *persons spoken to,* or
> *persons or things spoken about.*

First person stands for the person now *speaking:*

I got up early on Saturday morning.
sing.
   (*I*, the person speaking, is singular in number.)

We visited the Ryans yesterday.
pl.
   (*We*, the persons speaking, is the plural of *I*.)

Second person stands for the person *spoken to:*

> *You* are the one for me.
> sing.
> (*You*, the person spoken to, is singular.)

> *You* are the ones I want on our team.
> pl.
> (*You*, the persons spoken to, is the same pronoun for the plural as for the singular.)

Third person refers to a person or thing *spoken about:*

> *He* frequently writes to me.
> sing.

> *She* finally solved the puzzle.
> sing.

> *It* was an old Model-T Ford on display.
> sing.

> (*He* and *she*, the persons spoken about, are singular; and *it*, the thing spoken about, is also singular.)

> *They* enjoyed working on the farm together.
> pl.
> (*They*, the persons spoken about, is the plural of *he* and *she*.)

> I enjoy golf and tennis. *They* are my favorite outdoor sports.
> pl.
> (*They*, the things spoken about, is the plural of *it*.)

Exercise—Person and Number

Select the pronoun in each sentence. Classify the pronoun as to person and number. Follow the example.

EXAMPLE: We walked briskly to the lake.   (*We* is 1st person plural.)

1. I shall return soon.
2. They are innocent bystanders.
3. How can we fix the car?
4. When will she drive again?
5. Timmy, order whatever you want.
6. Maybe it doesn't cost too much.
7. You scouts are invited to camp.
8. Fair-weather friends I don't need.
9. Why blame it on the bus driver?

10. Thank you, Jack, for your thoughtful gift.
11. If we meet again, say hello.
12. With the paycheck she opened a savings account.
13. On the plane he carried a small bag.
14. At the checkpoint they inspected the contents.
15. Then he was allowed to board the plane.
16. Everything I said is the truth.
17. Let the bus come to a full stop before we get off.
18. At the signal she slowed down.
19. You girls look prepared to hike.
20. In parades they steal the show.

CASE OF PRONOUNS

Personal pronouns change form not only according to *person* and *number*, but also according to *case*—that is, how they are used in sentences. Except for *it* and *you*, a pronoun has one form when used in the *nominative case* and another form for the *objective case*. Memorize the pronouns in the following chart:

FORMS OF THE NOMINATIVE CASE AND THE OBJECTIVE CASE

	NOMINATIVE CASE		OBJECTIVE CASE	
Person	*Singular*	*Plural*	*Singular*	*Plural*
1st	I	we	me	us
2nd	you	you	you	you
3rd	he, she, it	they	him, her, it	them

USES OF THE NOMINATIVE CASE

1. The subject of a verb is in the nominative case.

   I rode the bike.

   <u>*Virginia* and *I*</u> went to the movies.

compound

   John is taller than *I*. (*am* is understood)

   Helen is as strong as *he*. (*is* is understood)

2. A pronoun that follows any form of the verb *to be* requires the same case as the subject of the verb.

Who is *she?* (not *her*)

It is *I.* (not *me*) (Conversation permits "It's *me.*")

3. A pronoun requires the same case as a noun with which it agrees.

WRONG: *Us* boys are going to the game.

RIGHT: *We* boys are going to the game.

(*We* is in the nominative because it agrees with *boys*, which is the subject.)

USES OF THE OBJECTIVE CASE

4. The direct object of a verb is in the objective case. The direct object is the receiver of the action.

The ball hit *me* (not *I*).

The ball hit <u>*Pablo* and *me*</u> (not *I*).
　　　　　　　　compound

5. The object of a preposition is in the objective case. (The prepositional phrases are underscored.)

The class sent the flowers <u>to *her*</u>.

The class sent flowers <u>to *Alice* and *her*</u>.
　　　　　　　　　　　compound

6. The indirect object is in the objective case.

The class sent *her* (not *she*) the flowers.

The class sent <u>*him* and *her*</u> (not *she*) the flowers.
　　　　　　　　compound

An indirect object is really a prepositional phrase with the preposition *to* or *for* understood.

The class sent <u>her</u> the flowers.	I left <u>*him*</u> a note.
indirect object	indirect object
The class sent <u>*to her*</u> the flowers.	I left <u>*for him*</u> a note.
prepositional phrase	prepositional phrase

7. A pronoun requires the same case as the noun with which it agrees.

WRONG: Give the books to *we* girls.

RIGHT: Give the books to *us* girls.

(*Us* is in the objective because it agrees with *girls*, which is the object of the preposition *to*.)

Exercises—Case of Pronouns

A. Write the pronoun that correctly completes the sentence.

1. John and (me, I) are friends.
2. Dinah drove Teresa and (me, I) to the theater.
3. (We, Us) students were detained after school.
4. It was (him, he) who spoke at the assembly.
5. Tony reads faster than (I, me).
6. This secret is between you and (I, me).
7. Jack joined Tom, Henry, and (I, me) in a practice game.
8. No one knew that it was (me, I).
9. Did you see (he, him)?
10. Aunt Tess gave Helen and (I, me) some good advice.
11. Louise and (her, she) played tennis.
12. Patricia introduced Maureen and (I, me) to her brother.
13. While playing, (us, we) girls found a ring.
14. I received a gift from Olga and (she, her).
15. It is doubtful if Miss Smith heard (we, us) girls.
16. I can swim as well as (her, she).
17. Uncle Henry wrote Terry and (she, her) a letter.
18. This is an ideal club for (us, we) girls.
19. Do you suppose it was (him, he)?
20. Do you believe (us, we) boys will win?

B. Write the pronoun that correctly completes the sentence.

1. Dad took Sam and (I, me) to the game.
2. It is (he, him) who broke the jar.
3. Can you call (him, he) to the phone?
4. (Us, We) girls must practice for the contest.
5. Helen is as tall as (her, she).
6. The money was divided between him and (I, me).
7. Aunt Ruth sent (he, him) a bike on his birthday.
8. Frank and (she, her) are cousins.
9. (Us, We) fellows should win the game easily.
10. Mr. Bates asked her and (he, him) to recite.
11. My father will call for Ramón and (I, me).

12. They dance better than (us, we).
13. The teacher was talking about you and (me, I).
14. The police praised (us, we) boys for our assistance.
15. I believe that (them, they) are the winners of the game.
16. Please give him and (I, me) a ride to the bus stop.
17. It is (her, she) who owns the canoe.
18. Did you call (him, he) today?
19. Sally sat down beside Anne and (me, I).
20. Do you believe Violet is older than (he, him)?

WHO AND WHOM

Although they are not personal pronouns, *who* and *whom* follow the rules of case. *Who* is the nominative form, and *whom* the objective.

1. Use *who* as a subject.
   Who gave you the ticket?

2. Use *whom* as a direct object.
   Whom will she marry?

3. Use *whom* as the object of a preposition.
   With *whom* are you going?

   HINT: Turn a sentence around when you are not sure of *who* or *whom.*

1. *Whom* will she marry?
   = She will marry *whom?*
     (*Whom* is the direct object of *will marry.*)

2. *Whom* are you voting for?
   = You are voting for *whom?*
     (*Whom* is the object of the preposition *for.*)

Exercise—*Who* and *Whom*

Write the pronoun that correctly completes the sentence.

1. (Who, Whom) called you?
2. (Who, Whom) do you prefer?
3. (Who, Whom) are you writing to?
4. (Who, Whom) is he?
5. For (who, whom) is this money?
6. (Who, Whom) did you send to the store?
7. (Who, Whom) should I give this to?
8. (Who, Whom) got the right answer?
9. To (who, whom) did you give the check?
10. (Who, Whom) is at the door?

POSSESSIVE CASE OF PERSONAL PRONOUNS

When used to show ownership or "belonging to" someone or something, the pronoun is said to be in the *possessive case*.

PRONOUNS IN THE POSSESSIVE CASE

	SINGULAR	PLURAL
1st person:	my, mine	our, ours
2nd person:	your, yours	your, yours
3rd person:	his her, hers its	their, theirs

Please notice that no apostrophe is used with the above pronouns because they are already in the possessive form!

Is this jacket *yours?* (not *your's*)

The land beyond the hedges is *theirs* (not *their's*).

That new, shiny sedan is *ours* (not *our's*).

Hers (not *Her's*) is a tan leather bag.

Wine left in an open bottle loses *its* (not *it's*) flavor.
(Remember: *it's* is the contraction for *it is*.)

NOTE: The possessive form of *who* is *whose*. Careless students write *who's*, which is the contraction for *who is*.

I feel sad for the family *whose* house burned down.
possessive

Who's the author of *Treasure Island?*
contraction

Exercise—Possessive Case of Pronouns

Write the correct form of the pronoun in each of the following sentences. Watch out for the apostrophe!

1. John Paul Jones said, "We have met the enemy, and they are (ours, our's)."
2. The land on the west bank used to be (their's, theirs).
3. The flag lost (its, it's) bright colors in the sun.

4. Teresa knew that the final reward would be (hers, her's).
5. A skateboard contest led to (his', his) accident.
6. If that dog is (yours, your's), teach him some manners.
7. The first half of the game was definitely (ours', ours).
8. I do not know (who's, whose) camera this is.
9. Have you watched the sunset with all (it's, its) colors?
10. Some Native American tribes are seeking settlements in the courts for the lands that were (theirs, theirs').

B. RELATIVE PRONOUNS

Relative pronouns are three: *who, that, which.* They are used to show the relation between a clause and some other word in the sentence. They differ in use, as follows:

> *who* is used for persons only
> *that* is used for persons or things
> *which* is used for animals or things, but never for persons

The candidate *who* (or *that* but not *which*) ran for mayor lived in our town.
        person

A car *that* starts in cold weather is my favorite.
    thing

The zoo keeper fed the bear cubs *which* were born in captivity.
                 animals

The capsule *which* (or *that*) took the astronauts to the moon returned to earth.   **thing**

Exercise—Review of Pronouns

Choose the correct pronoun in parentheses.

1. The Hamiltons, (who, which) moved in across the street, are from Jamaica.
2. Jeff and (I, me) play chess often.
3. That book on the front desk looks like (mine's, mine).
4. If (youse, you) have the time, will you go riding with me?

5. Children usually claim that the fault is not (theirs, their's).
6. These tomatoes are garden-grown and better than (ours, our's).
7. With (who, whom) are you going to the party?
8. The collie is the dog (which, who) barks at all strangers.
9. I am sure it was (he, him) who called you.
10. Pour the rest of the milk back into (it's, its) container.
11. Measure the size of the shoe to see whether (hers, her's) fits you.
12. The storekeeper created an important job for (she, her).
13. Aunt Anna invited Anita and (me, I) to her cottage for a long weekend.
14. The physician (which, who) used to be our family doctor has retired.
15. I can tell from the size (who's, whose) shirt this is.
16. Will you invite (us, we) girls to the picnic?
17. If it is (yours, your's), you should keep it in your closet.
18. When Alex fell from the ladder, he hurt (hisself, himself).
19. An insect (who, which) I detest is the spider.
20. When in trouble, (we, us) friends should stick together.

C. INDEFINITE PRONOUNS

Indefinite pronouns are called *indefinite* because they do not refer to a particular person or thing. Indefinite pronouns have number: most are singular; a few are plural.

The indefinite pronouns listed below are always singular and therefore require a singular verb.

SINGULAR PRONOUNS	SAMPLE SENTENCES
each	*Each* is going to bring lunch.
everything	*Everything* is more expensive than before.
anybody	Has *anybody* found the lost dog?
anyone	Was *anyone* interested in joining the Drama Club?
everybody	Has *everybody* finished already?
everyone	Nowadays *everyone* is watching the weather reports.
nobody	Was *nobody* prepared to speak?
none	*None* of them was wearing a uniform.
somebody	*Somebody* always leaves the window open.
someone	I believe *someone* has broken the lock.

The following indefinite pronouns are generally plural and take a plural verb.

PLURAL PRONOUNS	SAMPLE SENTENCES
some	*Some* of our students live near enough to walk home.
both	*Both* of the candidates have agreed to debate.
few	*Few* of the members were at the last meeting.
many	*Many* are leaving before the end.
several	*Several* of my friends live near me.

Exercise—Indefinite Pronouns

Write the correct word in each sentence.

1. (Is, Are) everybody in the cast present?
2. Both (is, are) good friends of mine.
3. Few of the athletes (looks, look) tired.
4. (Do, Does) anyone want to play ball with me?
5. (Is, Are) several of you going to walk home together?
6. Each (was, were) reading the music while playing.
7. As usual, nobody (has, have) offered to help clean up.
8. Many (are, is) eating lunch now.
9. At the meeting, everyone (were, was) present.
10. Will some of you boys (help, helps) me with these cartons?

ANTECEDENTS OF PRONOUNS

The *antecedent* of a pronoun is the word to which the pronoun refers.

Harold called *his* brother.
(antecedent)   pronoun

The *trees* have lost *their* leaves.
(antecedent)   pronoun

The antecedent, usually a noun, goes before the pronoun in the sentence. You will recognize the antecedent as the person, place, or thing originally mentioned, and then, following the antecedent, you will find the pronoun that stands for it.

Exercises—Antecedents of Pronouns

A. Write the pronoun in one column and its antecedent in a second column.

1. Alicia said that she could not swim to the raft.
2. Have the women begun their game?
3. New York is well known for its tall buildings.
4. Early in the morning, Phil filled his car with gas and drove to the beach.
5. Joe and Jill brought their tennis rackets.

B. Replace the blank with an appropriate pronoun.

1. California is famous for _____ abundant fruit crops.
2. We in the U.S.A. are glad to have Canada and Mexico as neighbors of _____.
3. Late in the evening, Morris typed _____ composition.
4. Have the carpenters started _____ work yet?
5. After lunch, Helen waxed _____ skis and headed for the hills.

AGREEMENT OF PRONOUNS WITH THEIR ANTECEDENTS

Agreement of pronouns with their antecedents means that a pronoun used in place of a noun must agree with the noun in person, number, and gender.

Person = 1st, 2nd, or 3rd. (Review pages 60–61.)
Number = singular or plural.
Gender = masculine, feminine, neuter, or common.

Common gender means that a noun may be either masculine or feminine; for example, *student*, *child*, *passenger*, *author*, etc.

Study these illustrations of pronouns agreeing with their antecedents in person, number, and gender.

1. *Thomas* lost *his* sneakers in the locker room.
   (antecedent)   pronoun

   (The pronoun *his* agrees with the noun *Thomas*, which is 3rd person, singular, masculine.)

2. *Mary*, give *your* dessert to Sara.
   (antecedent)   pronoun

   (The pronoun *your* agrees with the noun *Mary*, which is 2nd person, singular, feminine.)

3. Under the hot sun, the *ice cream* lost *its* texture.
                      (antecedent)   pronoun

(The pronoun *its* agrees with the noun *ice cream*, which is 3rd person, singular, neuter.)

4. We *citizens* are always obliged to pay *our* taxes on time.
   (antecedent)   pronoun

(The pronoun *our* agrees with the noun *citizens*, which is 1st person, plural, common).

INDEFINITE PRONOUNS AS ANTECEDENTS

On the previous pages, we discussed nouns as antecedents, but pronouns may also be antecedents. Consider the following sentence:

Somebody left (*his? her? their?*) jacket on the hook.

Which pronoun in parentheses would you choose as the correct answer? A common faulty choice is *their*. It is incorrect because *somebody* is singular and must be followed by a singular pronoun.

However, since you don't know whether the *somebody* is male or female, you cannot choose either *his* or *her* with certainty. Traditionally, the masculine was preferred when the gender was unknown. But today, more and more speakers choose *his or her* to include both possibilities. The correct choices then are

Somebody left *his* jacket on the hook.
  or:
Somebody left *his or her* jacket on the hook.

As we have learned, some indefinite pronouns are singular and some plural. (Review the distinctions on pages 68–69.) For example:

Everybody took *his or her* (not *their*) place on line.
sing.

If *anyone* wants to go to the bus stop, *he or she* (not *they*) may join us.
sing.

Many in the class did not understand *their* (not *his or her*) assignment.
pl.

Several asked for *their* (not *his or her*) money back.
pl.

Exercise—Agreement of Pronouns With Their Antecedents

Some sentences are faulty. If a sentence contains an incorrect pronoun, rewrite it correctly. For correct sentences, write C.

1. Ellen forgot to take her swimsuit.
2. Florida is famous for their oranges.
3. Has any one of the guests parked their car in the lot?
4. Ask Horace if his shoes need shining.
5. Both riders stopped and rested their horses.
6. Nowadays everything costs more than they used to.
7. Several of the answers do not match its questions.
8. Lena and Alice have already bought their tickets.
9. TV news has lost their interest for me.
10. Some of the actors knew his or her lines very well.
11. If everybody studied their part, we would not need a prompter.
12. Diners in a restaurant are responsible for its clothing.
13. Each of the stage "props" has its function in the play.
14. Hank's sister went to college when she was ten years old.
15. Many came late for his or her audition.
16. In the fall, trees begin to lose its leaves.
17. Someone raised their hand above the crowd.
18. Everybody should feel that his or her vote counts.
19. Myra asked Bill if she likes his new school.
20. Some workers in our factory bring its own lunch.

Exercise—Writing Pronouns

Can you supply the missing pronouns below?

1. Elena knew that __?__ couldn't swim underwater without __?__ snorkel.
2. Sponsors of TV programs want __?__ products advertised.
3. If elected, __?__ will become the first woman to hold that position.
4. Unlike his brother, __?__ likes to travel.
5. The captain of the team, a charming youngster, said __?__ name was Susan Campos.
6. All the dancers wore __?__ own native costumes.
7. The overhead train ride gave __?__ all a thrill.
8. How could __?__ admit that it was all my fault?
9. For a dollar, __?__ bought herself a new magazine.
10. In every crowd, somebody seeks __?__ lost friend.

Review of Pronouns

A. Supply the information required to complete the statements below.

1. A pronoun is a word used as a substitute for a __?__.
2. __?__ pronouns refer to persons.
3. The first person stands for the person __?__; the second person stands for the person __?__; and the third person refers to the person or thing __?__.
4. A pronoun used as the subject of a verb is said to be in the __?__ case.
5. A pronoun used as the object of a verb or of a preposition is said to be in the __?__ case.
6. Personal pronouns may be arranged in a chart to show the different forms that are required according to person, number, gender, and case. On your answer paper, draw such a chart as the one below and fill in the missing pronouns.

PERSONAL PRONOUNS

	SINGULAR		
	Nominative	*Objective*	*Possessive*
1st person:	I	?	my, ?
2nd person:	you	?	your, ?
3rd person:	he	?	?
	she	?	?, ?
	it	?	?
	PLURAL		
1st person:	we	us	?, ?
2nd person:	you	?	?, ?
3rd person:	they	?	?, ?

7. Relative pronouns are used to show the relation between a clause and some other word in the sentence. There are three: __?__, __?__, and __?__.
8. Pronouns ending in -*body*, -*one*, and -*thing* are always in the __?__ number.

9. Possessive pronouns—such as *ours, yours, hers, its,* and *theirs*—are already in the possessive form and therefore do not require an __?__ in spelling.

10. The antecedent of a pronoun is the noun or pronoun used somewhere before it in the sentence. The pronoun must agree with its antecedent in __?__, __?__, and __?__.

B. Rewrite each sentence correctly. Does each pronoun agree with its antecdent? Watch for pronouns and matching verbs!

1. It is her in the photograph.
2. Its too bad that us boys didn't take enough money with us.
3. Hardly anybody remembered to wear their raincoat.
4. The visiting team acted as though our court was their's.
5. The teacher said that none of the girls were at fault.
6. Even when us both knocked on the door, nobody answered.
7. The vendor which is at the door is selling eggs.
8. Its a bird of prey that snatches its food while in flight.
9. That swimming trophy was our's last year.
10. Emilio sat down on the bench between his brother and I.
11. We squeezed together to make some room for she and her friend.
12. He gave Don and I a slice of melon.
13. If everybody hands in their report on time, nobody will fail.
14. Each of the candidates have a sponsor to introduce them.
15. Does anybody want to check their answers now?

C. Classify the italicized pronouns according to person, number, gender, and case.

EXAMPLE: Tom forgot *his* wallet.
 PERSON: *3rd*   NUMBER: *sing.*   GENDER: *masc.*   CASE: *poss.*

1. Will *she* have enough money to go, too?
 PERSON: __?__   NUMBER: __?__   GENDER: __?__   CASE: __?__

2. The plane never altered *its* course in flight.
 PERSON: __?__   NUMBER: __?__   GENDER: __?__   CASE: __?__

3. The flight attendant offered *her* a blanket.
 PERSON: __?__   NUMBER: __?__   GENDER: __?__   CASE: __?__

4. Jane, carry *your* umbrella in case of rain.
 PERSON: __?__   NUMBER: __?__   GENDER: __?__   CASE: __?__

5. Some day *I* may travel to Japan.
 PERSON: __?__   NUMBER: __?__   GENDER: __?__   CASE: __?__

Chapter 8

Verbs

THE VERB EXPRESSES ACTION

A group of words without a verb stands still like a stalled car. Insert a verb and the sentence moves in the direction you want it to go. The verb is the engine that moves a sentence by giving it the power of meaning. For example, jot down a few groups of words without any verbs, like the following:

1. He __?__ against the wall.
2. The artist __?__ a marble statue.

What do they say? The meaning will depend on whatever verb you use, as illustrated below.

1. He *leaned* against the wall.
   He *stumbled* against the wall.
   He *scribbled* against the wall.
   He *stood* against the wall.

2. The artist *carved* a marble statue.
   The artist *bought* a marble statue.
   The artist *sold* a marble statue.
   The artist *designed* a marble statue.

Definition: **A verb is a word used to show action.** (See page 78 for a fuller definition.)

Exercise—Verbs

Write a different verb in each pair of sentences.

1. The bathers __?__ across the lake.
   The bathers __?__ across the lake.

2. The cook __?__ a special birthday cake.
   The cook __?__ a special birthday cake.

3. Four players __?__ on the athletic field.
   Four players __?__ on the athletic field.

4. The electrician __?__ the switch.
   The electrician __?__ the switch.

5. A nurse __?__ the cute little baby.
   A nurse __?__ the cute little baby.

6. Our home team __?__ another game yesterday.
   Our home team __?__ another game yesterday.

7. The victims of the flood __?__ financial aid.
   The victims of the flood __?__ financial aid.

8. A good doctor __?__ a nervous patient.
   A good doctor __?__ a nervous patient.

9. Some tired travelers __?__ a while.
   Some tired travelers __?__ a while.

10. A traffic officer __?__ the impatient drivers.
    A traffic officer __?__ the impatient drivers.

THE VERB TELLS THE STORY

You know that the verb is the heart of a sentence because it gives life and meaning to a group of words. In order to help you understand how really important the verb is in making sense, take any story (like the following one) and try to read it without the verbs. You will soon realize that a vital force is lacking.

Last spring, six of us —1— together in Spain. One day we —2— from Marbella to the famous Rock of Gibraltar. We —3— an ordinary car and after breakfast —4— on our way along the coast. We —5— the countryside beautiful, and the Spanish people —6— us with warm friendliness. At the port of Algeciras, we —7— a ferry across to the Rock because the border —8—. When we —9— inside the Rock, we —10— to discover enormous limestone caves which —11— by centuries of seeping water. At the top of the Rock, we —12— lunch in a restaurant from which we —13— Africa as well as Spain. On our way back, we —14— some peanuts to the apes in their tree house beside the road. With time and money, perhaps you, too, —15— this spot someday.

Answer Key: Here are the missing verbs. Other verbs are possible.

1. were vacationing	9. entered
2. drove	10. were surprised
3. rented	11. were caused
4. got started	12. ate
5. found	13. could see
6. treated	14. tossed
7. took	15. will travel to
8. was closed	

Exercise—Verbs in Sentences

Replace the word or words in parentheses with a verb selected from the list at the end of the exercise.

1. I am happy to (*receive*) this award.
2. How do they (*make by hand or machinery*) these plastic models of famous automobiles?
3. To face life's problems it is important to (*have faith*) in yourself.
4. After the ball game, the winners will (*have a good time*) their victory.
5. The astronauts were the first to (*find*) how to reach the moon safely.
6. Can you (*guess or picture in your mind*) how small our earth looks when you see it from far out in space?
7. The couple decided to (*tell publicly*) their wedding date.
8. A statesman once said, "He (*rules or controls*) best who (*rules or controls*) least."
9. A scientist is able to (*recognize*) samples of rocks, stones, and minerals.
10. In order to sell widely, companies (*print notices or broadcast*) their products or services.
11. "He who (*delays*) is lost."
12. The newlyweds (*supplied or equipped with necessary things*) their apartment in modern style.
13. After stepping on her toes, he (*said he was sorry*).
14. The Legal Aid Society will provide a lawyer to (*protect or guard*) the rights of an individual who needs help.
15. When a bank pays a customer's check, it (*marks paid or punches with holes*) the check.
16. Before issuing a notice to the students, you should ask someone in authority to (*give official permission*) it.
17. Just as in primitive times, music may be used to (*stimulate or arouse*) people's emotions.
18. Experience with real situations will (*train or develop*) you more than will books.
19. When the shadows (*grow longer*), we know that the sun is going down in the sky.
20. We usually (*close or end*) our meal with a choice of dessert.

VERB LIST

accept	believe	discover	hesitates
advertise	cancels	educate	identify
announce	celebrate	excite	imagine
apologized	conclude	furnished	lengthen
approve	defend	governs	manufacture

MAIN VERBS

There are two kinds of main verbs according to their use in sentences:

1. An **action verb** is a word that tells something which the subject does to another person or thing called the **object**.

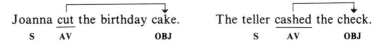

      Joanna cut the birthday cake.   The teller cashed the check.
      S   AV   OBJ   S   AV   OBJ

2. A **linking verb** (or **state-of-being verb**) is a word that describes a condition related only to the subject. The condition does not carry over to an object.

      My brother is an electrician.
      S   LV   N

      (*Electrician*, a noun, identifies the subject *brother*.)

      Margaret was happy over her grades.
      S   LV   ADJ

      (*Happy*, an adjective, describes the subject *Margaret*.)

The most common linking verb is *be*, which has various forms: *am, is, are, was, were,* etc.

Other linking verbs are the verbs of sensation. They include *look, feel, smell, taste, sound, seem, appear.*

      Mother seemed tired after the apple picking.
      S   LV   ADJ

      (The adjective *tired* describes the subject *Mother*.)

      They appear ready to take off now.
      S   LV   ADJ

      (The adjective *ready* describes the subject *They*.)

After a linking verb, look for a noun that identifies the subject or an adjective that describes the subject.

SUMMARY: A verb is a word that shows action or state of being. It is the heart of a sentence.

HELPING VERBS

A *helping verb* is a word used to help form the tense of a main verb. Examples: *be, do, can, have, will, may, was, did, could, had,* etc.

When a helping verb is used with a main verb, it is called a *verb phrase.* Examples:

> Thousands <u>were</u> thrilled by the World Series.
>   helper MV

> Next season we <u>may</u> buy tickets in advance.
>   helper MV

> Some players <u>will</u> always try to steal a base.
>   helper   MV

As you can see, the helping verb together with the main verb tells the time of the action or state of being. When you want to say something is now going on, you use the present tense of the helper:

> PRESENT TIME: It <u>is</u> raining today.
>   helper MV

When you want to form the past or the future tense in a sentence, use the past or future of the helper:

> PAST TIME: The worker <u>had</u> finished the job.
>   helper MV

> FUTURE TIME: Who <u>will</u> serve us breakfast?
>   helper MV

SUMMARY: **A helping verb is a word used to form the tense of a main verb.** Here are some examples:

HELPING VERB	+ MAIN VERB	= VERB PHRASE
have	been	have been
was	found	was found
could have	done	could have done
would have	passed	would have passed
may be	seen	may be seen
will be	employed	will be employed
did	return	did return
must have	followed	must have followed
should be	recognized	should be recognized
might have	escaped	might have escaped

Exercise—Helping Verbs

Write the correct form of the helping verb in each sentence. More than one way is possible as long as it makes good sense.

> EXAMPLE: Scientists claim the ice at the North Pole __?__ gradually melt. *Acceptable answers:* will, cannot, doesn't.

1. That was the worst accident we __?__ ever seen in our town.
2. She claimed that she __?__ drawn the portrait without help.
3. They felt they __?__ have been invited to the wedding.
4. Our parents __?__ allow us to go if we return by ten o'clock.
5. The newspaper __?__ have published the complete story.
6. Another tax __?__ drive more businesses out of our city.
7. The museum __?__ have shown the sculptures outdoors.
8. Our country __?__ face the serious problem of human relations.
9. When traveling abroad, you __?__ find most natives are friendly.
10. The fire fighters __?__ asked many questions about the fire.

REGULAR AND IRREGULAR VERBS

1. **Regular verbs** are different from irregular verbs in the way that they form their tenses. "What tense is the verb?" means "What time does the action take place?"

Regular verbs are so called because they follow a definite pattern in forming the present, past, and past participle.

Forming the Present Tense

There is no problem in forming the *pesent tense* because you simply drop the word "to" from the infinitive. For example, *to walk* becomes *I walk, you walk*, etc. This is true except in the third person singular which adds an *s* to the verb: *he walks, she walks, it walks.*

Forming the Present Participle

Forming the *present participle* is also easy and regular because you just add *ing* to any verb: *tell, telling.* Of course, you must be careful with certain verbs that make spelling changes whenever you add *ing: love, loving; swim, swimming.*

Forming the Past Tense and the Past Participle

The *past tense* and the *past participle* are formed by adding *ed*, *d*, or *t* to the present tense. However, the past participle requires a helping verb such as *have*, *has*, or *had*.

PRESENT	PAST	PAST PARTICIPLE
clean	+ *ed* = cleaned	(*have, has, had*) cleaned
use	+ *d* = used	(*have, has, had*) used
mean	+ *t* = meant	(*have, has, had*) meant

2. *Irregular verbs* are those verbs that form the past tense and the past participle in various ways other than by adding *ed*, *d*, or *t*. Here are a few examples to show how they are irregular.

	PRESENT	PAST	PAST PARTICIPLE
Change of ending:	*bend*	*bent*	(have, has, had) *bent*
Change of vowel:	*begin*	*began*	(have, has, had) *begun*
Change of vowel and consonant:	*leave*	*left*	(have, has, had) *left*

Note: A list of irregular verbs with their principal parts is printed on pages 82–83.

PRINCIPAL PARTS OF VERBS

The forms of the present tense, the past tense, and the past participle are the **principal parts** of verbs. Errors occur when misusing the past tense and the past participle. *Remember:* The past participle without a helper is a mistake.

Correct Use of the Past Tense

RIGHT: I <u>drank</u> (not *drunk*) a quart of milk.
      past
      tense

RIGHT: He <u>came</u> (not *come*) home late last night.
      past
      tense

RIGHT: She <u>did</u> (not *done*) her best on the test.
      past
      tense

Correct Use of the Past Participle

RIGHT: I have <u>drunk</u> (not *have drank*) a quart of milk.

> past
> participle

RIGHT: He <u>has come</u> (not *has came*) home already.

> past
> participle

RIGHT: She <u>had done</u> (not *had did*) her best on the test.

> past
> participle

Know the principal parts of verbs, and be sure to use the forms of the past tense and past participle correctly.

PRINCIPAL PARTS OF SOME TROUBLESOME VERBS

Present Tense	*Past Tense*	*Past Participle* (with *have, has, had*)
become	became	become
begin	began	begun
blow	blew	blown
break	broke	broken
burst	burst	burst
choose	chose	chosen
come	came	come
dive	dived, dove	dived
do	did	done
draw	drew	drawn
drink	drank	drunk
drive	drove	driven
eat	ate	eaten
fall	fell	fallen
fight	fought	fought
flee (to escape)	fled	fled
flow (a river flows)	flowed	flowed
fly (a bird flies)	flew	flown
forget	forgot	forgotten
freeze	froze	frozen
get	got	got, gotten
go	went	gone
grow	grew	grown

Present Tense	Past Tense	Past Participle (with *have, has, had*)
hang (things)	hung	hung
hang (persons)	hanged	hanged
know	knew	known
lay (to put down)	laid	laid
lead (to guide)	led	led
lie (to rest)	lay	lain
lie (to tell a lie)	lied	lied
raise (to lift)	raised	raised
ride	rode	ridden
rise (to ascend)	rose	risen
run	ran	run
say	said	said
see	saw	seen
set (to place)	set	set
sing	sang	sung
sit (to rest)	sat	sat
speak	spoke	spoken
swim	swam	swum
take	took	taken
teach	taught	taught
tear	tore	torn
throw	threw	thrown
wear	wore	worn
write	wrote	written

Exercises—Principal Parts of Verbs

A. Write the *past tense* form that makes the sentence correct.

1. A stranger (come, came) into our house.
2. Because of the freezing weather, the pipe (burst, busted).
3. I (run, ran) to school because I was late.
4. Somebody (laid, lay) my hat on the table this morning.
5. At the assembly this morning, we (sing, sang) patriotic songs.
6. Bill (done, did) it again, Mother.
7. Ann (lay, laid) the pot on the stove.
8. I (did, done) nothing to anger anybody.
9. Oscar (teached, taught) me to play chess.
10. I noticed the dog as he (laid, lay) on the porch.
11. A flock of birds (flewed, flew) in a V-formation.
12. Helen (hanged, hung) her dresses neatly in the closet.
13. After the third period, I (began, begun) to feel tired.
14. The juice was sour, but I (drank, drunk) it anyway.
15. I (seen, saw) him eat the cake.

B. Write the form of the *past participle* that makes the sentence correct.

1. Has she (ate, eaten) yet?
2. He has (drank, drunk) a pint of milk.
3. Robert had (fell, fallen) from his bike.
4. Nina has (took, taken) three lessons.
5. She has (did, done) her best.
6. She has just (gone, went) to school.
7. I have (written, wrote) my composition.
8. You should have (came, come) with us to the skating rink.
9. The dish had (fell, fallen) from the shelf.
10. I've (done, did) my homework.
11. Had you (saw, seen) this movie before?
12. The pitcher had (thrown, threw) the ball to first base.
13. Has Miguel (went, gone) to the store yet?
14. The general must have (wear, worn) all his medals.
15. She's (gone, went) there all by herself.

C. Complete these sentences by writing the proper form of the word in parentheses.

1. She has just (*go*) home.
2. Tom (*throw*) his hat on the bed.
3. Have you (*do*) your homework?
4. Ricardo (*drink*) two cups of coffee this morning.
5. The bottle of milk had (*fall*) to the floor.
6. Have you (*see*) my new watch?
7. Louise (*sing*) beautifully at the concert.
8. Has the mercury (*rise*) in the thermometer?
9. Paula has (*do*) the best work.
10. About an hour ago José (*go*) to the station.
11. We were (*teach*) first aid.
12. We (*ride*) in Uncle Joe's new car yesterday.
13. Have you (*speak*) to your Dad?
14. I have (*know*) Peter for five years.
15. Kay (*eat*) breakfast hurriedly and ran to school.
16. William had (*forget*) to buy the groceries.
17. We (*lay*) the dishes on the shelf.
18. We (*swim*) for an hour this morning.
19. He (*come*) home wet after the rain.
20. The bottle (*fall*) to the floor and burst.

TENSE

The *tense* of a verb refers to the time that an action or condition takes place: present, past, or future. It answers the question, "*When* did it happen?"

Present Tense

Use the *present tense* to express (1) something existing now or in process, (2) a general truth, and (3) an habitual action.

> We *are* both well again. (condition existing now)
> The rain *is falling* in buckets tonight. (something in process)
> A candle *makes* a cozy glow at the table. (general truth)
> "Pebbles" *barks* whenever a stranger approaches. (habitual action)

Past Tense

Use the *past tense* for an action or event that was completed in past time.

> I *wrote* him a friendly note yesterday.
> Those *were* the good old days.
> Scriptures say, "Out of the void *came* the heavens and the earth."

Future Tense

Use the *future tense* to describe an event that will be completed at a time yet to come. The future tense is formed by using *shall* or *will.*

> Some day we *shall travel* to the Rocky Mountains.
> You *will enjoy* a vacation at the seashore.
> They *will take* a cruise to the Bahamas next week.

Clues regarding tense are provided by certain *time* words or phrases like the following:

last year	yesterday	before
a week ago	some time ago	later
once upon a time	at that time	earlier
now	tomorrow	bygone days
today	next year	days to come

Exercise—Time Words Suggest the Tense of Verbs

Rewrite each sentence using the correct verb in parentheses. Then underline the time word or phrase.

1. A hundred years from now, do you think all our homes (were heated, will be heated) by the sun's energy.
2. Do you remember what you (ate, eat) for breakfast this morning?
3. Young people must demand the halt to pollution because they (did inherit, will inherit) the earth some day.
4. A Chinese proverb says, "A journey of a thousand miles (begins, began) with a single step."
5. Before electronic toys were introduced, we (will play, used to play) outdoor games.

SEQUENCE OF TENSES

When a sentence contains two clauses, it is necessary to show the proper relationship between these two clauses. Something happens in one clause and another thing happens in the other clause. Did they occur at the same time? Did one come first? The right tense in each clause will show the actual time sequence. **The *sequence of tenses* means the order of time expressed by the verbs.**

CORRECT: He *ate* because he *was* hungry.
    past   past

CORRECT: She *smiled* when they *met*.
    past   past

CORRECT: Since it *is* late, we *are going* to bed.
    present   present

CORRECT: Galileo *believed* the earth *goes* around the sun.
    past   present
        (general truth)

CORRECT: We *hope* our friends *will come* early.
    present   future

Faulty Changes in Sequence of Tenses

An unnecessary shift of tense from past to present or from present to past results in confusion of time. These faulty changes are due to carelessness. Study the following pairs of sentences in order that you may avoid this kind of blunder in your own writing.

1. WRONG: She *took* a piece of cake, and then she *starts* to eat it when no
   past   present
   one was looking.

   RIGHT: She *took* a piece of cake, and then she *started* to eat it when no
   past   past
   one was looking.

2. WRONG: He *drove* up to the house, and quickly he *honks* his horn to
   past   present
   call his friend.

   RIGHT: He *drove* up to the house, and quickly he *honked* his horn to
   past   past
   call his friend.

3. WRONG: Wanderers *say* they are living just for today, but they *forgot*
   present   past
   that it is necessary to work and save for tomorrow.

   RIGHT: Wanderers *say* they are living just for today, but they *forget*
   present   present
   that it is necessary to work and save for tomorrow.

4. WRONG: While Barbara *is* putting in her contact lenses, her friend
   present
   Janet *came* running upstairs.
   past

   RIGHT: While Barbara *is* putting in her contact lenses, her friend
   present
   Janet *comes* running upstairs.
   present

Exercise—Sequence of Tenses

Choose the correct form of the verb in parentheses, paying attention to the sequence of time between ideas.

1. The highway patrol discovered some cars stalled on the turnpike; they (moved, moves) them off the road.
2. The doctor (ordered, orders) aspirin and plenty of fluids for the patient who suffered from a bad cold.
3. When he lost his job, he (starts, started) to become a drifter.

4. Early travelers to Alaska found a territory that (is, was) rich in minerals but lacking in people.
5. We once offered every customer who (will buy, bought) a TV set a ninety-day guarantee.
6. The oceans contain tons of minerals which (wash, will wash) down from rivers and streams.
7. Health foods like raisins and prunes cost more than they (use to, used to).
8. We rely on the National Guard that (defends, defended) us in case of attack.
9. Coupons attract bargain hunters, but low prices (are, will be) better.
10. We enjoy a cruise ship, but we (eat, ate) too much food.

AGREEMENT OF SUBJECT AND VERB

Agreement means that the subject and verb must be alike in number. A singular subject requires a singular verb, and a plural subject requires a plural verb.

Joan of Arc was the leader of the armies of France.
      sing.   sing.

The seven *dwarfs were* in Disney's SNOW WHITE.
      pl.   pl.

This may seem simple and easy. It is not. This business of making the verb agree with its subject is one of the most common causes of student errors. Just listen to your friends on the bus, at the ball game, in the cafeteria, or anywhere else. Do you hear expressions such as these?

QUICK QUIZ

Can you spot the errors in these sentences? Check your answers with those on the next page.

1. They was making a lot of noise on the bus yesterday.
2. We was sitting near the fifty-yard line at the game.
3. I thought you was somewhere up in the grandstand.
4. One of the original paintings were sold at auction.
5. Marion don't want to discuss the problem.
6. Everybody sitting at the tables were having lunch.
7. The foreign stamps across the package was very valuable.
8. José or she are tutoring Luis after school.
9. Here is the road maps I promised you.
10. Measles are an annoying childhood disease.

Answers:

1. They *were* making a lot of noise on the bus yesterday.
2. We *were* sitting near the fifty-yard line at the game.
3. I thought you *were* somewhere up in the grandstand.
4. One of the original paintings *was* sold at auction.
5. Marion *doesn't* want to discuss the problem.
6. Everybody sitting at the tables *was* having lunch.
7. The foreign stamps across the package *were* very valuable.
8. José or she *is* tutoring Luis after school.
9. Here *are* the road maps I promised you.
10. Measles *is* an annoying childhood disease.

GUIDELINES FOR AGREEMENT OF SUBJECT AND VERB

1. If the subject is *I, he, she, it*—use a *singular* verb.
   If the subject is *we, you, they*—use a *plural* verb.

SINGULAR	PLURAL
I *am* going home. He *is* older than John. She *was* dressed in blue. It *was* raining yesterday.	We *are* friends. You *were* absent. They *were* surprised.

Notice: You always takes a *plural* verb even if only one person is addressed. Never say *you is* or *you was* or *youse.*

You *are* (not *is*) a good student.
You *are* good students.

2. Be careful in using *don't* and *doesn't* to match the subject.

WRONG	RIGHT
He *don't* know the answer. She *don't* feel well. It *don't* matter at all.	He *doesn't* know the answer. She *doesn't* feel well. It *doesn't* matter at all.

Notice: Doesn't means "does not" and always takes a *singular* subject. *Don't* means "do not."

RIGHT

I *don't* know the answer.   We *don't* want dessert.
You *don't* look well this morning.   They *don't* hear us.

3. When a phrase (underlined below) comes between the subject and the verb, be sure to make the verb agree with the subject. You can spot the subject word by omitting the phrase.

> *One* of the boys *is* trying to blow up a balloon.
> *One* (_____) *is* trying to blow up a balloon.

> The *bus* with all its passengers *was* rolling down the street.
> The *bus* (_____) *was* rolling down the street.

4. When two or more subject words are joined by *and*, they generally take a *plural* verb. The subject is called a **compound subject** because it contains more than one noun or pronoun.

> Mary and Francine *are* sleigh riding in the park.
> (compound subject)

> He and I   *are* going to join the stamp club.
> (compound subject)

5. When two or more subject words are connected by *or, either . . . or, neither . . . nor,* or *nor,* the verb agrees with the nearer subject. The position makes the difference. (The subject words are underlined below.)

> *Either* the dry spell *or* the insects make the plants wilt.
>   sing.   pl.   pl.

> *Neither* the farmers *nor* nature overcomes such disaster.
>   pl.   sing.   sing.

6. Some indefinite pronouns, including the following, are always singular and require a singular verb: *one, none, anyone, anybody, someone, somebody, everyone, everybody, everything, no one, nobody, each, another, either, neither.*

> Nobody *is* able to sell cars for less money.
> *Has* anyone seen my jacket?
> Somebody *doesn't* like peanut butter sandwiches.
> Each of his books *has* a neat label on it.
> Everyone with a ticket *is* admitted at the gate.

7. Some indefinite pronouns are generally plural and require a plural verb: *both, few, many, several, most.*

> Both *are* acting in the play.
> Few of our classmates *were* late this morning.
> Several in the crowd *were* injured.

8. When a sentence begins with the introductory word *There* or *Here*, look for the subject following the verb. That is, the order is V-S. Then decide whether the verb should be singular or plural to match the subject. Remember that *There's* is a contraction for *There is*, and *Here's* is short for *Here is*.

> WRONG: There's only two pieces of cake left.
> RIGHT: There <u>are</u> only two <u>pieces</u> of cake left.
>   V   subject

> WRONG: Here's the pen and paper you asked for.
> RIGHT: Here <u>are</u> the <u>pen and paper</u> you asked for.
>   V   compound subject

9. Some nouns spelled with a final *s* look plural but are considered singular: *news, measles, civics, mathematics, politics, athletics*. Therefore, they require a singular verb.

> Good news *is* always welcome.
> Mathematics *is* my favorite subject.
> Politics *is* a career in government.
> Athletics *builds* school spirit.

Exercises—Agreement of Subject and Verb

A. Write the correct form of the verb in parentheses, making sure it agrees with the subject.

 1. Either you or your friends (is, are) to blame for the accident.
 2. (There's, There are) no shortcuts to fame and fortune.
 3. You (was, were) the only one missing from our lunch table.
 4. Neither Barbara nor Sara (do, does) homework on Saturdays.
 5. Hilda and Greta (is, are) trading block issues of stamps.
 6. (Here's, Here are) the directions for getting to the ball park.
 7. There (was, were) herds of elephants scattered through the plains.
 8. Both the doctor and her nurse (come, comes) to work on foot.
 9. The vice-president or the treasurer (is, are) holding the meeting.
10. Where (has, have) the children gone?

B. Write the correct form of the verb in parentheses, making sure it agrees with the subject.

 1. The veteran with all his medals (were, was) honored by the town.
 2. Books of adventure (is, are) popular with teenagers.
 3. Two women in Bob's office (play, plays) tournament tennis.
 4. The person on the steps (are, is) leaning on the handrail.
 5. The sound of the sirens (are, is) frightening at night.

6. All members of the team (was, were) invited to the victory celebration.
7. The plane with its crew (are, is) trying to take off now.
8. Dad with his cronies (like, likes) to play a little poker.
9. Stores around my school (sell, sells) school supplies.
10. Sam with two helpers (clean, cleans) the store every day.

C. Write the correct form of the verb in parentheses, making sure it agrees with the subject.

1. I hope everybody (have, has) studied the lesson.
2. I expect somebody else (have, has) read a different story.
3. Down in the tropics, it (don't, doesn't) snow except on mountaintops.
4. None of the programs (is, are) free from station breaks.
5. The Bible says, "Many are called but few (is, are) chosen."
6. In the morning, she (don't, doesn't) feel like eating.
7. Most of the streets (was, were) cleared of snow by nightfall.
8. Good news (travel, travels) slow, but bad news fast.
9. Wealth or fame (don't, doesn't) impress me.
10. I think politics (is, are) a good career for able lawyers.

CHOOSING VERBS TO STRENGTHEN THE MEANING OF A SENTENCE

A verb can tell more than *what* happened; it can suggest *how* it happened. Colorful, active, vivid verbs strengthen the meaning of a sentence.

1. He *tasted* it.

Did he nibble at it, swallow it whole, smack his lips, gulp it down, guzzle it, devour it, gorge it, try it on the tip of his tongue, relish it?

2. She *said* something.

Did she whisper it, mutter it, mumble it, shout it, yell it, scream it, speak softly, state it positively, utter it clearly?

3. You should *ask* first.

Should you question politely, interrogate, query, inquire, quiz, examine, beg, plead, request, implore, beseech, appeal, or pray?

The ordinary or colorless verbs *say*, *ask*, *taste*, and others used every day have become outworn. If you look in the dictionary or a book of synonyms, you will find some other verbs that will help you to say whatever you want. Thus, your speaking and writing will gain power, variety, and flexibility.

Exercise—Colorful Active Verbs

Using the dictionary and your imagination, replace the ordinary or color-less verbs with colorful active verbs.

1. We *walked* home in the dark.
2. The train *arrived* at the station.
3. A stone *broke* the window of the car.
4. The truck *drove* around the corner.
5. The shoppers *went* to the bargain counter.
6. An angry lion *looked* out of his cage.
7. The hungry boy *ate* the food.
8. The rain *came* down in the forest.
9. The high tide *rolled* over the rocks.
10. Suddenly, the church bells *rang*.
11. We *smelled* the food cooking on the grill.
12. Our parents *saw* us diving in the pool.
13. The customer *touched* the garment.
14. Next morning, the sun *rose*.
15. Although it was early in the evening, the stars *were shining*.

HOW TO FORM A VERB BY ADDING AN ENDING TO A WORD

When you study the way words came into the English language, you will find that we have borrowed heavily from Latin, Greek, and French. Therefore, you will notice that our verbs end in suffixes which help to carry the meaning. Look up the dictionary definitions of the examples below and study the verb endings (or suffixes) in order that you may recognize verbs and guess their meanings. Example: short + *en* = shorten ("to make short"). So, you can figure out other words having *en* (*fatten, hasten, blacken*, etc.).

VERB ENDING	MEANING	EXAMPLES
-ate	make, or do	captivate, stimulate, regulate
-en	make, or become	whiten, lengthen, quicken
-it	make, or do	edit, merit, inhabit
-er	do, or act	flutter, glimmer, spatter
-fy	make, or do	liquefy, magnify, beautify
-ish	act, or do	publish, nourish, finish
-ise	make, or treat	advertise, surprise, improvise
-ite	make, or treat	unite, excite, invite
-ize	make, or do	sterilize, theorize, modernize
-le	cause, or make	sparkle, dribble, wriggle

Exercises—Verb Endings

A. Using the verb endings listed previously, write the complete verbs.

1. advert _ _ _
2. cultiv _ _ _
3. bright _ _
4. antagon _ _ _
5. cack _ _
6. humidi _ _
7. suffoc _ _ _
8. van _ _ _
9. improv _ _ _
10. mer _ _
11. abbrevi _ _ _
12. bapt _ _ _
13. exagger _ _ _
14. fright _ _
15. ed _ _

16. fin _ _ _
17. penal _ _ _
18. ling _ _
19. ign _ _ _
20. nibb _ _
21. agit _ _ _
22. tight _ _
23. comprom _ _ _
24. inhab _ _
25. incorpor _ _ _
26. start _ _
27. pun _ _ _
28. glitt _ _
29. whit _ _
30. scandal _ _ _

B. Each group of verbs listed below uses a certain ending. Look up the meanings of the verbs in each group, but try to figure out the meanings before you check with the dictionary. Remember that -ate, -fy, -ize mean "make, or do."

-ATE	-FY	-IZE
concentrate	amplify	agonize
fascinate	clarify	apologize
venerate	dignify	slenderize
perpetuate	electrify	deodorize
celebrate	fortify	emphasize
accommodate	gratify	fraternize
graduate	modify	harmonize
emancipate	petrify	magnetize
speculate	specify	nationalize
terminate	testify	socialize

Exercise—Verbs in Sentences

Write the correct verb, chosen from the list above, that fits the meaning of each sentence below.

1. If you turn off the radio, you can (*give your full attention*) on the work you are doing.
2. Will you please (*make clear*) the reason for planting beans in rows?

3. It takes real courage to (*express regret*) for your misbehavior sometimes.
4. They say that Chinese youngsters (*pay respect to*) their elders as a family courtesy and tradition.
5. When using a spray can to (*remove odors*), be careful not to aim toward someone's face or eyes.
6. On February 12 we usually have a holiday from school in order to (*pay honor*) Abraham Lincoln's birthday.
7. The barons during the Middle Ages used to (*build forts and battlements*) their castles against invaders.
8. Our coach likes to (*make important*) certain points by showing us how to shoot for the basket.
9. If you are willing to take a risk with your extra money, you may decide to (*buy or sell with the chance of gain or loss*).
10. We had a group of friends who used to like to (*sing together*) around the piano.
11. In order to bring together children of all kinds in the schools, the mayor decided to (*furnish space or seats for*) pupils from nearby areas.
12. Before a witness may (*give evidence*) in court, he or she must swear on the Bible to tell the truth.
13. Education provides opportunities for youngsters to (*share experiences together*) in a friendly atmosphere.
14. A pink slip in a pay envelope may contain an official notice to (*end*) employment.
15. An extra check, or bonus, serves to reward good work and (*make glad*) the employee.

Review of Verbs

A. Complete the following statements correctly.

1. A verb is a word used to __?__ or __?__.
2. Verbs such as these (*eat, study, work*) are called __?__ verbs.
3. Verbs such as these (*be, have, do*) are called __?__ verbs.
4. Two or more helping verbs used with a main verb form a verb __?__.
5. Regular verbs form the past tense by adding __?__, __?__, or __?__ to the present tense.
6. Verbs that form the past tense by changing the spelling of the present tense are called __?__ verbs.
7. Words such as *last year, yesterday, a week ago* are clues that the verb will be in the __?__ tense.
8. Words such as *now, today, this very moment* are clues that the verb will be in the __?__ tense.
9. Expressions such as *next week, hereafter, tomorrow* are hints that the verb will be in the __?__ tense.
10. "Agreement" means that the subject and the verb in a sentence must be alike in __?__.
11. If the subject is *you* (referring to one or more persons), the verb must be __?__ in number.
12. When there are two subjects joined by *and*, the verb must be __?__ in number.
13. Pronouns such as *anybody, someone, nobody* are always __?__ in number and require a __?__ verb.
14. Some pronouns such as *both, few, most* are always __?__ in number and require a __?__ verb.
15. Some nouns (*news, athletics, politics*) spelled with a final *s* look plural but are considered __?__ in number; therefore, they require a __?__ verb.
16. To strengthen the meaning of a sentence, you should replace ordinary or colorless verbs (such as *say, ask, do*) with colorful active verbs (such as __?__, __?__, __?__).
17. The endings (or suffixes) *-ate, -fy, -ize* mean that the verb has the general meaning of __?__, as in *terminate, magnify, realize*.

B. Write the correct form of the verb required to complete the meaning in each of the following sentences.

1. You should have (*see*) my brother Peter in his Halloween costume.
2. Thelma (*go*) home some other way.
3. Who has (*do*) harm to our garden?
4. Only inspired men of God could have (*write*) the marvelous books of the Bible.

5. The outfielder (*throw*) the ball straight to home plate to stop the run.
6. The officer must have (*drive*) the patrol car about ninety miles an hour to catch the bank robbers.
7. The check had been (*draw*) on a local bank, but the manager refused to cash it.
8. The neighbors should have (*know*) that the Gaffneys were out of town because the newspapers had piled up.
9. What strange scent has (*lead*) the tiger to the homemade trap?
10. In faraway places, women, too, have (*fight*) for the cause of freedom and democracy.
11. I should have (*speak*) with greater kindness, but I felt too angry with her at the time.
12. The leading soprano in the choir had (*sing*) the melody in order to have the rest of us follow her.
13. What evil star must have (*rise*) in the skies on that fateful morning?
14. Mom's heart would have (*break*) if that antique vase had fallen when the mover stumbled.
15. The refugees from the island (*swim*) at least two miles to reach the safety of the mainland.
16. She should have (*wear*) slippers to avoid splinters.
17. Mike has (*sit*) out in the broiling sun just to get a suntan.
18. At the height of the storm, the wind (*blow*) the big billboard down across the highway.
19. In cleaning out the slums, the wrecking crew should have (*tear*) down not only the buildings but the ancient prejudices, too.
20. We hope that someday all the people of the earth will have (*forget*) their differences and recognized the brotherhood of man.

C. Rewrite the following sentences by changing the tense of the verbs from present or future to past time.

1. Carlotta comes into the room, looks around, and says hello.
2. The dog wags its tail as it runs toward the trainer.
3. The bank adds interest on my account which I keep on deposit at least three months.
4. A mother expecting obedience gives directions to her children who still live with the family.
5. Where are the boys and girls who fill the house with laughter?
6. Why do the growing years bring so much anxiety?
7. The music on the radio is so noisy that it makes your eardrums grow less sensitive to sound.
8. If you go to the movies, you will find more violence.
9. All of us appreciate the soft voice and the kind word that brighten our lives.
10. Who among all your friends is willing to do for you what only your parents do?

D. Choose the correct form of the verb in parentheses.

1. When Bess and Angela (sing, sings) the harmony, the song sounds great.
2. Either state or federal funds (is, are) needed to improve transportation.
3. There (was, were) no good news on TV tonight.
4. Both snapper and pompano (are, is) delicious Florida fish.
5. Everybody (has, have) left for the school outing.
6. Had I known (you, youse) fellows were coming, I'd have waited awhile.
7. Neither the teeth nor the mouth (seem, seems) to be drawn well.
8. Mother, (here's here are) the fruit and vegetables you ordered.
9. Our star quarterback (don't, doesn't) know whether he can play tomorrow.
10. (Has, Have) anyone a dime for the phone?
11. Don't you think Jack and Jill (make, makes) a fine couple?
12. There (is, are) no shoes like old shoes for comfort.
13. Everyone in the stands (applaud, applauds) when Reggie comes to bat.
14. Certain products from Japan (have, has) taken the lead in market sales.
15. A collection of trophies (hang, hangs) from the crosspiece.

E. Use more colorful verbs to show the action! Depending on the desired effect, all three verbs are acceptable here! Justify *your* choice.

EXAMPLE: A tiny salamander (scooted, darted, skidded) __?__ like a shot across the garden path. (Answer: *darted*)

1. A lonesome dog (howled, whined, barked) __?__ as if in pain.
2. A yellow bird hidden in the tree (trilled, sang, caroled) __?__ with rippling notes.
3. Petruchio never (begged, pleaded, implored) __?__ on bended knee.
4. Kate usually (replied, retorted, responded) __?__ with biting sarcasm.
5. The blimp slowly (soared, zoomed, climbed) __?__ above the clouds.
6. The stolen car (skidded, caromed, jolted) __?__ around the corner as it fled from the pursuers.
7. A beautiful seashell was (tossed, carried, washed) __?__ ashore by the rolling waves.
8. A genuine ruby (shines, gleams, glows) __?__ with a red fire.
9. The music of a piano and a violin help (accompany, support, enrich) __?__ the vocalist's performance.
10. Strong wind followed by heavy rain (altered, affected, damaged) __?__ our plans for outdoor dining.

Chapter 9

Modifiers: Adjectives and Adverbs

Sketch a house and trees in the rough. Then add some specific details. *Modifiers* are the details that make the picture clear!

BARE SENTENCE: There was a house among the trees.

WITH MODIFIERS: There was a *neat little* cottage with a *pointed* roof
                                       adj.   **adj.**   **adj.**

                 standing *quietly* among the *leafy* trees.
                             adv.   **adj.**

(ADJECTIVES: *neat, little, pointed, leafy;* ADVERB: *quietly*)

WHICH PICTURE IS CLEARER? WHY?

When you try to describe somebody, you use words that suggest certain qualities about the way the person looks or acts. You may give size, shape, age, or general appearance. You use words that give specific details to build an impression or picture. Surely, you have heard such expressions as

tall, *dark*, and *handsome* man
young, *petite*, and *beautiful* woman
slim, *sweet*, and *charming* child

The words in italics are called **modifiers** because they are used to fix more clearly what somebody looks like. Since they are used to modify a noun (*man*, *woman*, *child*), they are **adjectives**.

When you want to explain how something is done, you use words that describe the way it is done. You may refer to speed, time, place, manner, or general action.

Slowly, *quietly*, *cautiously* she opened the door.
Suddenly, *angrily*, *violently* he slammed it shut.

These words ending in *ly* serve to tell the manner in which the action was done. They are **adverbs** because they modify the verb (*opened*, *slammed*).

DEFINITIONS

A **modifier** is any word used to describe or limit the meaning of another word. (A modifier is either an adjective or an adverb.)

An **adjective** is a word used to describe a noun or a pronoun. It answers the questions: *which one? what kind? how much? how many?* etc.

This book is yours. (answers *which one?*)
I bought a *red* sweater. (answers *what kind?*)
Three inches of rain fell yesterday. (answers *how much?*)
Several students started the petition. (answers *how many?*)

An **adverb** is a word used to describe a verb, an adjective, or another adverb. It answers the questions: *how? when? where? in what manner?*

This pen writes *smoothly*. (answers *how?*)
We will play soccer *tomorrow*. (answers *when?*)
I looked *everywhere* for you. (answers *where?*)
She shouted *angrily* at him. (answers *in what manner?*)

POSITION OF ADJECTIVES

An adjective usually *precedes* the noun or pronoun that it modifies.

the *tall* man   the *new* car
the *slim* woman   the *old* building

Adjectives sometimes *follow* the word they modify in order to make a stronger impression.

Americans used to prefer cars *big, roomy*, and *powerful.*
Foreigners like cars *small, cozy*, and *efficient.*

When the adjective is placed after a linking verb and modifies the subject, the adjective is called a **predicate adjective.** (Review *linking verbs*, page 78.)

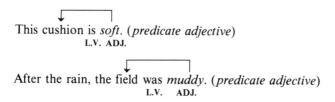

This cushion is *soft.* (*predicate adjective*)
                L.V.   **ADJ.**

After the rain, the field was *muddy.* (*predicate adjective*)
                      L.V.   **ADJ.**

However, if the adjective modifies a noun in the predicate, it is *not* a predicate adjective.

This is a *soft* cushion.   The result was a *muddy* field.
         ADJ.   **ADJ.**

Exercise—Adjectives as Modifiers

Select the adjective in each sentence and write the word that the adjective modifies.

EXAMPLE: I heard a loud noise in the basement. (*Loud* modifies *noise.*)

1. A cold wind came out of the north.
2. Over the hills dark clouds gathered.
3. Lobster is abundant in Maine.
4. We roasted plump chestnuts in the fire.
5. On New Year's Eve, Times Square is very crowded.
6. A circle of happy faces stared at the flame.
7. Someone started to sing old favorites.
8. Gasoline was scarce during the strike.
9. I like the smell and smoke of a wood fire.

10. Togetherness helps make easy friendships.
11. It was a glorious day for a picnic.
12. The leader told us a ghost story.
13. We toasted marshmallows on a broken twig.
14. When it grew late, we went to bed.
15. Alfred was nervous when he began his speech.

ADJECTIVES MODIFY NOUNS

When adjectives modify nouns they sometimes travel together in pairs or trios in order to give more details in building a stronger image. A lonely noun is a vague thing. A noun with two or three adjectives comes clearly into focus as a picture. Take an ordinary noun all by itself and then add a few adjectives. What a difference!

NOUN	+	ADJECTIVES
bread		a slice of *buttered, toasted* bread
snow		a pile of *slushy, dirty* snow
penny		a *bright, new, shining* penny

Exercise—Adjectives (Two in a Row)

A. Write the adjective that completes the phrase. Notice the definition given in parentheses.

1. deep and d___k (black) secret
2. crisp and c_____y (chewy) cereal
3. lank and l___n (thin) cowboy
4. sweet and l_____y (pretty) girl
5. small and p_____e (not public) wedding
6. rock and r___l (swinging) music
7. tired but h____y (satisfied) picnickers
8. tattered and t___n (ripped) jeans
9. sick and t____d (worn-out) actors
10. slow but s___e (certain) progress

B. Write complete sentences using these phrases.

1. high and mighty
2. neat and tidy
3. young and strong
4. footloose and fancy-free
5. cold and terrified
6. cruel and savage
7. kind and loving
8. airtight and waterproof
9. strange and unexpected
10. good-humored and mischievous

Exercise—Adjectives (Three in a Row)

Write the word that completes the series of three adjectives.

1. tall, dark, and h _ _ _ _ _ _ _ e (attractive) man
2. short, fat, and u _ _ y (unattractive) fellow
3. dull, dark, and d _ _ _ _ _ y (drab) afternoon
4. long, sleek, and s _ _ _ _ y (gleaming) car
5. clean, fresh, and f _ _ _ _ _ _ _ t (fresh-smelling) linen
6. bright, warm, and s _ _ _ _ y (brilliant) morning
7. healthy, wealthy, and w _ _ e (sensible) person
8. soft, smooth, and s _ _ _ _ y (delicate) skin
9. ready, willing, and a _ _ e (skillful) worker
10. gay, sparkling, and f _ _ _ y (amusing) comedienne

ADJECTIVES USED AS COMPLEMENTS OF THE VERB

There is a special group of verbs which are followed by adjectives in order to complete the meaning of the sentence. These verbs refer to the five senses and to the state of being:

to be	to look
to seem	to taste
to become	to smell
to grow	to feel
to appear	to sound

In each of the sentences below, the verb says something about the subject. The adjective rounds out the statement by completing the verb and at the same time qualifying the subject. Study the following illustrations that show adjectives (*not* adverbs) used as complements of the verb.

1. Your handwriting looks *neat*. (not *neatly*)
2. A slice of watermelon tastes *sweet* and *juicy*.
3. Freshly picked flowers smell *fragrant*.
4. A fur collar feels *soft* against your cheek.
5. A fire gong sounds *alarming* and *exciting*.
6. The little baby was *cute* and *attractive*.
7. Some of the girls seemed *sleepy* during the movie.
8. Perhaps some day you may become *famous*.
9. After playing baseball, Louis grew quite *tired*.
10. The certificate appears *authentic*.

Exercise—Complements

A complement completes the meaning of a verb. Complements are the *direct object*, *indirect object*, *predicate adjective*, *predicate noun*.

Frank hit a <u>homer</u>.

D.O.

Dad gave <u>me</u> a <u>dollar</u>.

I.O.   D.O.

The fish smells <u>terrible</u>.

P.A.

My brother is a <u>teacher</u>.

P.N.

Write the complements in these sentences and label each as D.O., I.O., P.A., or P.N.

1. We toured the Rockies last summer.
2. Martha feels too tired to skate now.
3. My sister offered Harold a ride to school.
4. Thomas Edison was the inventor of the dictating machine.
5. Salads taste better with dressing.
6. With her savings, Alice bought a home computer.
7. Tell me the purpose of the meeting.
8. After our long walk, the suggested rest at the coffee shop sounded good to us.
9. Tom has been our best pitcher this season.
10. Please give me another slice of turkey.
11. Did you find your keys?
12. The store purchased a new delivery truck.
13. The waiter handed us the dinner menu.
14. "Does the price seem right?" Horace asked.
15. Mrs. Rodriguez has become a dietician.

POSITION OF ADVERBS

An adverb usually follows the verb that it modifies. Nearness makes the meaning instantly clear.

She spoke *quickly*.
Friends contributed *generously*.
The hospital bill was paid *promptly*.

An adverb may interrupt a verb phrase. This serves to emphasize the way something occurs.

The deer had *almost* reached the edge of the woods.
The hunter has *only* wounded the doe.
It must have *lightly* snowed during the night.

Sometimes an adverb begins a sentence.

Obviously, no one is at fault.
Certainly, we are all friends here.
Besides, nothing really matters.

As you can see from these sample sentences, the adverb moves about quite freely in the beginning, the middle, or the end of a statement. The important point to remember is that it must be clear to the listener or reader which word it modifies. Avoid such misplacing of adverbs as the following:

He *only* came to argue.
(*Better:* He came *only* to argue.)

She *even* didn't answer.
(*Better:* She didn't *even* answer.)

It broke their friendship *almost*.
(*Better:* It *almost* broke their friendship.)

ADVERBS MODIFY VERBS, ADJECTIVES, OTHER ADVERBS

Adverbs are words used to make clear the limits of the words they modify. Adverbs either enlarge or reduce the scope of a word. For example:

Modify Verbs

The guests ate *sparingly*.   (a little food)
The guests ate *hungrily*.   (a lot of food)

Modify Adjectives

The runners looked *slightly* weary.   (a bit tired)
The runners looked *very* weary.   (worn out)

Modify Other Adverbs

The champion *always* scored easily.   (every time)
The champion *never* scored easily.   (at no time)

Adverbs usually refer to time, place, manner, or degree.

> We heard the news *later.* (time)
> The youngster ran *home.* (place)
> The announcer spoke *precisely.* (manner)
> These muffins look *almost* burnt. (degree)

Summary: Learn to use adverbs whenever you want to pinpoint the way things happen or people behave.

Exercise—Adverbs as Modifiers

In each sentence, select the adverb and then label the word that it modifies.

EXAMPLE: The boxer swung wildly. (*Wildly* modifies swung.)

1. The referee blew the whistle loudly.
2. The opponent staggered blindly to his corner.
3. Meanwhile, the crowd roared.
4. Some customers angrily booed.
5. The bell rang and the round promptly ended.
6. The ring was almost surrounded by reporters.
7. Cameras flashed continuously it seemed.
8. The fight promoters split the profits evenly.
9. The boxers were terribly battered.
10. They hardly earned enough to heal their wounds.
11. The new film made very good photographs.
12. Time for developing and printing was much shorter.
13. Were those giants really stronger than men?
14. Despite their size, they moved quite rapidly.
15. The Little League accepts players rather young.
16. The first frost chilled our garden too soon.
17. The visiting team played almost desperately.
18. Don't handle a puppy so roughly.
19. Feed the birds in spring more generously.
20. Riding the air currents, the birds fly less effortlessly.

ADVERBS FORMED FROM ADJECTIVES

Some adverbs are formed by adding *ly* to adjectives.

ADJECTIVE + LY = ADVERB

bad + ly = badly
nice + ly = nicely
quick + ly = quickly

Caution: Whenever you add *ly* to an adjective ending in *l,* be careful to spell the adverb correctly (double *l*).

accidental + ly = accidentally
cruel + ly = cruelly
incidental + ly = incidentally

Practice spelling these adverbs formed from the adjectives.

occasional + ly =   beautiful + ly =   equal + ly =
intentional + ly =   careful + ly =   actual + ly =
annual + ly =   cordial + ly =   doubtful + ly =

Remember this: Adjectives modify nouns: *tall* ship, *cold* steel, *warm* smile. Adverbs modify verbs (sailed *calmly*), adjectives (*very* eager), and other adverbs (*more* seriously).

Notice: Some words ending in *ly* are adjectives: a *lovely* day, a *friendly* person, a *sickly* child.

Exercise—Adverbs Formed From Adjectives

Write the word that completes the sentence correctly.

1. Pat shouted, "You just dented my fender very (bad) _?_!"
2. A police officer quite (calm) _?_ reported the accident.
3. The company settled the account somewhat later and (reluctant) _?_.
4. Northerners are flocking to the Caribbean islands (eager) _?_ seeking sun and fun.
5. Sometimes the (real) _?_ bright students may not score well on tests.
6. A slow learner may develop ability (surprising) _?_ late in life.
7. The skater skimmed across the ice very (skillful) _?_.
8. I regret your recent mishap very (sincere) _?_.
9. Some farmers spoke (rude) _?_ when grain was boycotted.
10. The room was very (plain) _?_ decorated.

HOW TO DISTINGUISH BETWEEN ADJECTIVES AND ADVERBS

A word may be used in one sentence as an adjective and in another sentence as an adverb. Take the word *early*. It is used as an adjective in the sentence, "The *early* bird catches the worm." Here *early* modifies the noun *bird*. However, it is used as an adverb in the sentence, "He arose *early* to see the sunrise." In this sentence, *early* modifies the verb *arose*. Note well: The use of a word determines its part of speech.

Exercise—Adjective or Adverb?

In each pair of sentences below there is a word used as an adjective in one sentence and as an adverb in another sentence. Can you explain their different uses?

1. *a.* The late students reported to the office for a pass.
   b. The boys who came late had to stay after school.
2. *a.* Those who shout loudest have the wrong answers.
   b. The loudest complainers have no real cause for grievance.
3. *a.* A slow trickle of blood showed where the razor cut him.
   b. As the battery wore out, the kitchen clock ran *slow*. (= slowly)
4. *a.* She used a sharp pair of scissors to cut the material.
   b. The game began at eight o'clock *sharp*. (= punctually)
5. *a.* One of the blessings of town living is fresh water on tap.
   b. The milk came fresh from the cow.

USING ADJECTIVES AND ADVERBS TO STRENGTHEN SENTENCES

The skeleton of a sentence consists of two or three principal words used as subject, verb, and object. For example: "Go home!" "The girl won a scholarship." "The boy ate the cake." "The hunter killed the deer." In order to give a fuller picture of what happened, you need to supply adjectives and adverbs that round out the meaning. Ask yourself these questions: *what kind? in what manner?* The answers to these and other questions will provide you with enough adjectives and adverbs to cover the skeleton of each sentence with the flesh of meaning.

1. girl—won—scholarship
2. boy—ate—cake
3. hunter—killed—deer
4. artist—painted—scene
5. scientist—discovered—cure
6. actor—told—stories
7. pilot—flew—plane
8. team—won—trophy
9. storekeeper—sold—articles
10. collector—bought—antiques

Exercise—Forming Adjectives and Adverbs

On each line below are a suffix and a word (an adjective or an adverb) which ends with that suffix. Write two additional words for each suffix.

SUFFIX	ADJECTIVE OR ADVERB	SUFFIX	ADJECTIVE OR ADVERB
1. able	lovable	9. ly	slowly
2. al	national	10. most	topmost
3. en	golden	11. ce	twice
4. er	colder	12. ward	homeward
5. est	warmest	13. long	sidelong
6. ful	delightful	14. wise	likewise
7. ish	clownish	15. way	anyway
8. ious	glorious		

PROPER ADJECTIVES

Proper adjectives are formed from proper nouns and must always be spelled with a capital letter. Proper adjectives commonly refer to countries.

COMMON NOUN	PROPER NOUN	PROPER ADJECTIVE
country	Canada	Canadian

SUFFIXES OF SOME PROPER ADJECTIVES

-ish: English, Irish, Turkish
-an: Roman, Mexican, German
-ese: Chinese, Portuguese, Vietnamese
-ian: Indian, Australian, Italian

RADICAL CHANGES IN SPELLING OF SOME PROPER ADJECTIVES

PROPER NOUN	PROPER ADJECTIVE
Greece	Greek
France	French
Denmark	Danish
Netherlands	Dutch
Switzerland	Swiss

Exercise—Proper Adjectives

Write the adjective that corresponds to each of the following countries.

1. Canada	6. Turkey	11. Denmark	16. Portugal
2. France	7. Brazil	12. Russia	17. Italy
3. England	8. Sweden	13. China	18. Greece
4. Spain	9. Switzerland	14. Japan	19. Mexico
5. Africa	10. Norway	15. Poland	20. Germany

COMPARISON OF ADJECTIVES

When we compare persons or things in order to see which contains more or less of a certain quality, we express this relationship in three ways:

- POSITIVE—denotes the simple quality.
    Henry is a *tall* boy. Ann is a *short* girl.

- COMPARATIVE—denotes a higher or lower degree of the quality.
    Charles is a *taller* boy. Lena is a *shorter* girl.

- SUPERLATIVE—denotes the highest or lowest degree of the quality.
    Peter is the *tallest* boy. Irma is the *shortest* girl.

FORMING THE DEGREES OF COMPARISON

REGULAR ADJECTIVES

Adjectives of One Syllable

Add *er* to form the comparative and *est* to form the superlative.

POSITIVE	COMPARATIVE	SUPERLATIVE
neat	neater	neatest
strong	stronger	strongest
cold	colder	coldest

Adjectives of Two Syllables

Either way (*er, est* or *more, most*) is acceptable for some adjectives.

POSITIVE	COMPARATIVE	SUPERLATIVE
easy	easier or more easy	easiest or most easy
sleepy	sleepier or more sleepy	sleepiest or most sleepy
mighty	mightier or more mighty	mightiest or most mighty

Adjectives of Two or More Syllables

These usually take *more* and *most*.

POSITIVE	COMPARATIVE	SUPERLATIVE
cautious	more cautious	most cautious
joyful	more joyful	most joyful
natural	more natural	most natural
dangerous	more dangerous	most dangerous
challenging	more challenging	most challenging

Just as *more* and *most* express a greater degree of a quality, so *less* and *least* denote a lesser degree. For example:

> joyful, *more* joyful, *most* joyful
> joyful, *less* joyful, *least* joyful

Never use both methods of comparisons together.

> prettier, prettiest (not *more* prettier, nor *most* prettiest)
> sweeter, sweetest (not *more* sweeter, nor *most* sweetest)

Use the comparative degree when two persons or things are compared, and the superlative degree when more than two persons or things are compared. The superlative degree usually requires *the* (*the* most handsome boy).

> Of my *two* sisters, Ramona is *less* (not *least*) studious.
> John is the *oldest* (not *older*) of the *three* boys.

Study the following list of irregular comparisons.

IRREGULAR ADJECTIVES

POSITIVE	COMPARATIVE	SUPERLATIVE
bad	worse	worst
far	farther, further	farthest, furthest
good	better	best
ill	worse	worst
little	less	least
many	more	most
much	more	most
old	older, elder	oldest, eldest

Exercise—Degree of Comparison

Write the word in parentheses that makes the sentence correct.

1. My dog is the (more, most) playful of the three.
2. Tom is the (more, most) capable member of the swimming team.
3. Mary is the (taller, tallest) of the two girls.
4. Anne is (prettier, more prettier) than her sister.
5. Evelina is the (stronger, strongest) of the two.
6. This flower is the (larger, largest) of the two.
7. Is George a (better, more better) player than Henry?
8. Mrs. Smith is a (stricter, more stricter) teacher than Mr. Jones.
9. This is the (swiftest, more swiftest) river I have ever seen.
10. Florence is the (more, most) capable student in the class.
11. Mr. Big is the (most richest, richest) man in town.
12. This one is the (least, less) attractive of the two hats.
13. This piece of candy is the (sweetest, most sweetest) in the box.
14. My drawing was the (bestest, best) in the school.
15. I got a (more better, better) mark than Sam.
16. Olga is the (smartest, smarter) of the three sisters.
17. Of the two teams, I like this one (best, better).
18. John's composition was the (most, more) interesting in the class.
19. Susan is the (less, least) mischievous of the four children.
20. This picture is (more pretty, prettier) than that one.

Exercise—Comparison of Adjectives

Write the comparative and the superlative of each of the following adjectives.

1. pretty	8. beautiful	14. lovely	20. sleepy
2. good	9. bright	15. much	21. old
3. quick	10. shiny	16. adventurous	22. little
4. useful	11. tall	17. tired	23. small
5. early	12. happy	18. clean	24. lonely
6. bad	13. smart	19. swift	25. intelligent
7. easy			

COMPARISON OF ADVERBS

Most adverbs form the comparative and superlative degrees in the same way as adjectives, by adding *er* for the comparative and *est* for the superlative.

1. Adverbs of one syllable form the comparative degree by adding *er*, and the superlative degree by adding *est*.

ONE-SYLLABLE ADVERBS

POSITIVE	COMPARATIVE	SUPERLATIVE
long	longer	longest
short	shorter	shortest
fast	faster	fastest
loud	louder	loudest
near	nearer	nearest
far	farther	farthest
hard	harder	hardest
late	later	latest
quick	quicker	quickest

2. Adverbs ending in *ly* form the comparative with *more* and the superlative with *most*.

POSITIVE	COMPARATIVE	SUPERLATIVE
beautifully	more beautifully	most beautifully
cleverly	more cleverly	most cleverly
wisely	more wisely	most wisely
nobly	more nobly	most nobly
cheaply	more cheaply	most cheaply

IRREGULAR ADVERBS

POSITIVE	COMPARATIVE	SUPERLATIVE
well	better	best
much	more	most
little	less	least
badly	worse	worst

Exercise—Comparison of Adverbs

Write the comparative and the superlative degrees for each of the following adverbs. Review the rules to help you!

1. lively	6. near	11. badly	16. little
2. safe	7. cleverly	12. late	17. promptly
3. slowly	8. loud	13. much	18. well
4. quick	9. happily	14. wisely	19. sincerely
5. cheaply	10. far	15. nobly	20. beautifully

NEGATIVE WORDS

Negative means "no." The negative words are *no, not, nobody, nothing, none, never, hardly, scarcely, barely, only, but* (meaning *only*).

It is wrong to use two negatives in a row because one cancels out the other. One negative does the job!

WRONG: *Nobody can't (cannot) do it.*
                 (*nobody* and *cannot* = double negative)
RIGHT: *Nobody can do it.* (single negative)

WRONG: *I can't (cannot) hardly lift it.*
                 (*cannot* and *hardly* = double negative)
RIGHT: *I can hardly lift it.* (single negative)

AVOID DOUBLE NEGATIVES

Say He did*n't* say *anything* (not *nothing*).
  or He said nothing.

Say I do*n't* like *any* (not *none*) of these hats.
  or I like none of these hats.

Say I could*n't* go *anywhere* (not *nowhere*).
  or I could go nowhere.

Say We did*n't* see *anybody* (not *nobody*).
  or We saw nobody.

Say You *can* (not *can't*) *hardly* tell them apart.
  or You can't tell them apart.

Say She *is* (not *isn't*) *barely* able to walk.
  or She isn't able to walk.

Say We *were* (not *weren't*) *scarcely* able to hear.
  or We weren't able to hear.

Say The child *could* (not *couldn't*) *hardly* write.
  or The child couldn't write.

Exercises—Double Negatives

A. Write complete sentences using a single negative word.

1. not
2. nobody
3. nothing
4. none
5. never
6. hardly
7. scarcely
8. barely
9. only
10. but (meaning *only*)

B. In each of the following sentences, select the word in parentheses that makes the sentence correct.

1. I didn't hear (nothing, anything).
2. She did not have (anything, nothing) to do.
3. I couldn't see (no, any) way to help her.
4. I can't find my book (anywhere, nowhere).
5. You (can, can't) scarcely tell it from the original.
6. They do not need (no, any) help.
7. I (could, couldn't) hardly talk.
8. I don't see him carrying (no, any) packages.
9. It (was, wasn't) barely noticeable.
10. Of all the suits I saw, I didn't like (none, any).
11. He (can't, can) hardly walk a block.
12. We didn't meet (nobody, anybody) but Florence.
13. We didn't see (any, no) lights in the house.
14. Harry didn't talk to (nobody, anybody).
15. We (weren't, were) scarcely able to sleep.
16. I didn't see (none, any) of my friends.
17. You (can't, can) hardly tell the difference.
18. Isn't there (anything, nothing) you want to read?
19. Let's not go (anywhere, nowhere).
20. You won't find (none, any) there.
21. I (was, wasn't) barely able to move.
22. We saw many boats, but I didn't buy (none, any).
23. Wasn't (no one, anyone) at home?
24. She didn't have (no, any) time to spend.
25. Don't you have (nothing, anything) to say?

Review of Adjectives and Adverbs

A. Supply the information required to complete the statements below.

1. A modifier is a word used to __?__ .
2. An adjective is a word used to modify a __?__ .
3. An adverb is a word used to modify a __?__ , an __?__ , or another __?__ .
4. In this sentence, all the modifiers are called __?__ : "An illegal act deserves proper punishment."
5. In this sentence, all the modifiers in italics are called __?__ : "This shoe polish cleans *quickly*, removes stains *easily*, and provides a shine *beautifully*."
6. An adjective that follows a linking verb and relates to the subject is a __?__ adjective. Example: The ocean was *calm*.
7. When the adverbial ending *ly* is added to an adjective ending in *l* (like *usual*), there will be __?__ l's before the *y*.

B. Some words may be used in a sentence either as adjectives or as adverbs, depending on their relation to the word they modify. Write *adj.* or *adv.* for each italicized word.

1. At the red light, you may not go *forward*.
2. Sometimes the *dark* horse wins the race.
3. When making your speech, don't speak too *loud*.
4. You lose the petals when you pick a *full-blown* rose.
5. A *rusty* nail may cause an infection.

C. Compare these adjectives:

POSITIVE	COMPARATIVE	SUPERLATIVE
1. good	__?__	__?__
2. __?__	less	__?__
3. __?__	__?__	furthest
4. strong	__?__	__?__
5. __?__	richer	__?__
6. __?__	__?__	most capable

D. Compare these adverbs:

POSITIVE	COMPARATIVE	SUPERLATIVE
1. well	?	?
2. ?	?	worst
3. cheaply	?	?
4. ?	more friendly	?
5. ?	?	most wisely

E. Avoid double negatives! Rewrite these sentences, omitting the unnecessary words.

1. She wasn't barely able to be heard in the room.
2. There weren't none but the relatives of the bride.
3. We couldn't scarcely walk home after the hike.
4. The newlyweds couldn't hardly pay for the furniture.
5. He wouldn't do nothing unless he was paid first.

F. Supply an adjective complement for each sentence below.

1. In a few years these youngsters will become __?__.
2. On a cold morning, hot chocolate tastes __?__.
3. I really hope that you will soon feel much __?__.
4. With her new Easter bonnet, doesn't she look __?__?
5. The ringing of the burglar alarm sounded __?__.

G. Write complete sentences using these proper adjectives.

1. Spanish   2. French   3. Italian   4. Chinese   5. Russian

H. In the sentences below, distinguish between *good* and *well*. Use *good* as an adjective and *well* as an adverb.

1. The radio does not sound (good, well).
2. Gloria has always done her lessons (good, well).
3. My hands are so cold I can't write (good, well).
4. Emma does not swim as (good, well) as Edna.
5. We ate (good, well), but the food didn't taste so (good, well).

I. Write the adjective or the adverb that makes the sentence correct.

1. Cross the streets (careful, carefully).
2. Why did you stop so (sudden, suddenly)?
3. Because she lost her pen, Helen felt (badly, bad).
4. Ethel recited the poem very (nervous, nervously).
5. The rose smells (sweet, sweetly).
6. Father seemed very (thoughtful, thoughtfully).
7. She shouted very (angrily, angry).
8. We strolled along (aimless, aimlessly).
9. The sun appeared very (bright, brightly).
10. Elena spells very (bad, badly).
11. Pat spoke very (strange, strangely).
12. The burning rubber smelled (badly, bad).
13. His voice sounded (gruff, gruffly).
14. Delia was late; so she dressed very (quick, quickly).
15. The lawn looked (beautiful, beautifully).

J. Write the adjective that correctly completes the sentence.

1. On a hot summer day, the beach is (cooler, more cooler) than the city.
2. I got the (best, bestest) mark in the class.
3. Elaine is the (younger, youngest) of the three children.
4. Fred is the (least, less) dependable member of the club.
5. Of all the houses on the street, the dentist's is the (beautifulest, most beautiful).

Chapter 10

Prepositions and Conjunctions

Connections hold things together. A wristwatch is tied around your wrist with a band or linked chain. A long line of freight trains is connected by coupling devices. All the bones in your body are connected by tissues. The members of your family are connected by name and by blood. Wherever you look, you see connections!

In the classroom, the overhead lights are connected by electric cables. The faucets in the sink are connected by pipes to the plumbing system. In a similar way, the ideas in a sentence may be joined together by connecting words called *prepositions* and **conjunctions.**

WHY DO WE NEED PREPOSITIONS AND CONJUNCTIONS?

Try reading these sentences without the connecting words.

1. When batting, keep your eye the ball.
2. Next time put your money your pocket.
3. Please leave the rear exit.
4. He felt better soon he had the tooth pulled.
5. She got home just they served dinner.
6. The front bell rang no one opened the door.

Now, notice the connecting words showing relationships.

1. When batting, keep your eye *on* the ball.
   prep.
2. Next time put your money *in* your pocket.
   prep.
3. Please leave *by* the rear exit.
   prep.
4. He felt better soon *after* he had the tooth pulled.
   conj.
5. She got home just *before* they served dinner.
   conj.
6. The front bell rang, *but* no one opened the door.
   conj.

A. PREPOSITIONS

PREPOSITIONS CONNECT IDEAS

A *preposition* is a word that connects a noun or pronoun with some other word in a sentence.

The colors *of* our flag are red, white, and blue.
(The preposition *of* relates *flag* to *colors*.)

We bought a new car *with* air conditioning.
(The preposition *with* relates *air conditioning* to *car*.)

Violet and I walked *over* the bridge.
(The preposition *over* relates *bridge* to *walked*.)

I wrote a letter *to* her.
(The preposition *to* relates *her* to *wrote*.)

PREPOSITIONS SHOW RELATION BETWEEN IDEAS

A preposition not only connects ideas but also shows the relation between them. For example, a preposition may show—

DIRECTION: toward, behind, from, around
Where did she go? She ran *toward* the door.

TIME: before, after, during, while
When will she return? She will come back *after* lunch.

POSITION: on, under, over, inside
Where are his books? He left them *on* the desk.

CAUSE: due to, on account of, because of
Why did he forget them? It was *due to* his carelessness.

SOME COMMON PREPOSITIONS

A handy list of everyday prepositions used to link ideas together includes the following:

about	below	in	through
above	beneath	inside	to
across	beside	into	toward
after	between	like	under
against	beyond	near	underneath
along	by	of	until
among	down	off	up
around	during	on	upon
at	except	out	with
before	for	outside	within
behind	from	over	without

Exercise—Prepositions

Write an appropriate preposition for each of the following sentences. In some sentences, more than one preposition may fit the meaning.

1. I left my watch __?__ the table.
2. Alice sent a birthday card __?__ me.
3. As I rose __?__ my chair, my heart beat __?__ a heavy hammer.
4. __?__ noon, the painters stopped working.
5. Sacramento is the capital __?__ California.
6. __?__ the soil are the roots of a tree; __?__ the ground is the trunk.
7. I whistled __?__ him, but he paid no attention __?__ my call.
8. We watched the passing parade __?__ my window.
9. An ambulance drove __?__ the street, and the lights shone __?__ my face.
10. He claimed he was innocent __?__ the crime, but he acted __?__ a criminal.
11. __?__ England, a subway is called an underground.
12. He stuck his hat __?__ his head, and stalked __?__ the door.
13. All the South American countries __?__ Bolivia and Paraguay have access to the sea.
14. The spacecraft *Voyager 2* will travel __?__ the outer planets of our solar system.
15. Some papers blew __?__ the room and landed __?__ the wall.

PREPOSITIONAL PHRASES

The word *preposition* comes from the Latin *pre* meaning "before" and *posit* meaning "to place." The preposition is placed before a noun or pronoun which is called the **object of the preposition.** The preposition and the object of the preposition together are called a **prepositional phrase.**

A list <u>of candidates</u> was posted.
prep. phrase

This letter is <u>for you</u>.
prep. phrase

The object of the preposition may have modifiers.

All members <u>of the football team</u> reported for practice.
prep. phrase

An accident occurred <u>at the dangerous intersection</u>.
prep. phrase

Exercise—Prepositional Phrases

Copy the sentence. Then underline each prepositional phrase. Double underline the preposition, and circle the object of the preposition.

1. Let's practice some basketball in the school playground.
2. After a short delay, the game resumed.
3. Type your composition on plain white paper.
4. Near the old red schoolhouse a fire started.
5. She was competing against very strong rivals.
6. By your actions we will judge your character.
7. The child ran down the hill and fell.
8. Among the contestants, he was chosen the winner.
9. The explorers beat a path through the Amazon jungle.
10. Toward nightfall they gave up the search.
11. Give me a hand with these heavy cartons.
12. Upon my honor I told the truth.

B. CONJUNCTIONS

WHAT IS A CONJUNCTION?

A *conjunction* is a word used to connect words, phrases, or clauses. When it joins these word groups together, it also shows their relationship in meaning. It makes a thought connection as well as a grammatical linking of parts. The word *conjunction* comes from the Latin *con* ("together") + *junct* ("join"); therefore, conjunction means "joining together."

WHAT DOES A CONJUNCTION DO?

1. **A conjunction connects *words:***

    He ate meat *and* potatoes.
    She prefers vanilla *or* strawberry.
    Lincoln was poor *but* honest.

2. **A conjunction connects *phrases:***

    The Navy has power in the air *and* on the sea.
    Was it taken from your coat *or* from your locker?
    Tell her to take it out of the oven *but* keep it in the baking pan.

3. **A conjunction connects *clauses:***

    She showed some trophies *that* she had won in golf and bowling.
    <u>main clause</u>   <u>dependent clause</u>

    She helped in the campaign *because* she was willing to learn.
    <u>main clause</u>   <u>dependent clause</u>

    They peeled potatoes *and* we helped set the table.
    <u>main clause</u>   <u>main clause</u>

Conjunctions make the sense or meaning clear by making the connections between ideas according to the intention of the speaker or writer. The conjunction is the missing link in the following sentences. Which one fits best?

He explored the cave *but* / *although* / *since* / *because* / *after* he found no buried treasure.

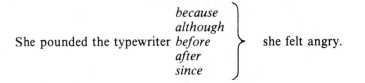

$$
\text{She pounded the typewriter}
\left.\begin{array}{l}
\textit{because} \\
\textit{although} \\
\textit{before} \\
\textit{after} \\
\textit{since}
\end{array}\right\}
\text{she felt angry.}
$$

Your choice of conjunction makes a difference in the meaning.

TWO KINDS OF CONJUNCTIONS

A *coordinate conjunction* joins two main clauses (or independent clauses) in order to show that the ideas carry equal value in the sentence. The most common coordinate conjunctions are *and, or, but.*

They went skating, *and* we went bowling.
    main clause   main clause

You may buy stocks, *or* you may invest in real estate.
    main clause   main clause

He enlisted as a private, *but* he retired as a general.
    main clause   main clause

A *subordinate conjunction* joins a main clause with a dependent clause (or subordinate clause). The conjunction shows the relationship between ideas expressed according to time, purpose, condition, manner, comparison, contrast, or result.

Words frequently used as subordinate conjunctions are:

after	how	that	when	while
as	if	then	whenever	who
as if	since	though	where	whoever
because	so	unless	whereas	why
before	so that	until	whether	yet

Since supper is ready, let's go inside and eat.
    dependent clause

Speak louder *so that* everyone may hear you.
        dependent clause

Good neighbors welcomed us *when* we moved here.
        dependent clause

PHRASE AND CLAUSE DISTINGUISHED

Some words serve as conjunctions and at other times as prepositions. The difference depends on whether the connected group of words is a clause or a phrase.

as
- CONJUNCTION: The bus arrived on time *as* we expected.
  <u>clause</u>
- PREPOSITION: His word was good *as* gold.
  <u>phrase</u>

while
- CONJUNCTION: Fred grew impatient *while* he waited for service.
  <u>clause</u>
- PREPOSITION: The quarterback was injured *while* playing.
  <u>phrase</u>

Do you notice the difference between a clause and a prepositional phrase?

A *clause* contains a subject and a predicate.

A prepositional *phrase* contains a preposition and a noun or pronoun, but lacks a subject and a predicate.

Exercise—Conjunctions

Write the appropriate conjunction required to complete the sentence.

1. About five o'clock __?__ the sun went down, we lowered the flag.
2. I really don't know __?__ I can go to the game tomorrow.
3. Don't pay the bill __?__ you have received the goods.
4. The girl waved good-bye, __?__ her mother did not see her.
5. Our income has risen, __?__ our standard of living has gone up.
6. The weather looks __?__ it is about to change for the better.
7. Why not take the medicine just __?__ the doctor prescribed.
8. Basil told them __?__ he was once able to chin twenty times.
9. We don't mind __?__ you do the job as long as it is done.
10. Be prepared to go __?__ your choice of careers will take you.
11. Check your addition __?__ you settle the account.
12. There is no use feeling sorry __?__ the vase is shattered on the floor.
13. Is there a beach in the Virgin Islands __?__ palm trees grow?
14. Why not visit Venice __?__ it is a short distance from Rome?
15. You should travel widely __?__ it broadens your experience with people.

16. Will you please tell me __?__ I can solve this problem?
17. She kept on practicing __?__ she felt certain she would win the voice contest.
18. Some musicians have talent __?__ others have mechanical skill.
19. The ones who care are the ones __?__ finally make it.
20. Should I telephone tonight, __?__ send a letter tomorrow?

ERRORS TO AVOID IN USING PREPOSITIONS AND CONJUNCTIONS

1. Omit extra prepositions!

WRONG: How did the story end *up?*
RIGHT: How did the story end?

WRONG: Where have you been *at?*
RIGHT: Where have you been?

WRONG: The man to whom I gave it *to* was my uncle.
RIGHT: The man to whom I gave it was my uncle.

2. Notice the correct usage of certain words often confused.

a. **among** is used when referring to more than two
between is used when referring to two

RIGHT: The money was divided *between* two charities.
RIGHT: The box of candy was shared *among* all the pupils.

b. **beside** means "next to"
besides means "in addition to"

RIGHT: Stand *beside* her.
RIGHT: She invited her friends *besides* all her relatives.

c. **angry *at*** refers to a thing
angry *with* refers to a person

RIGHT: I was *angry at* the resolution passed by the students.
RIGHT: I was *angry with* the coach for breaking his promise.

d. **could of, must of, should of, would of** are all WRONG
could have, must have, should have, would have are all RIGHT

RIGHT: You *should have* gone to the dentist a month ago for a checkup.

> *Note:* The misuse of *of* for *have* arises from the fact that in spoken English we usually slur the sound of *have*, as in "You should've gone."

e. **in** means "already within"
into means "from outside"

RIGHT: Diana jumped in the water. (She just moved around while already *within*.)
RIGHT: Diana jumped into the water. (She dived into it from *outside*.)

f. **off** suggests "removing something on"
from suggests "taking something away"

RIGHT: He took *off* his coat.
RIGHT: I borrowed the book *from* (not *off of*) him.

g. **different from** is correct American usage
different than is British usage

RIGHT: Doreen looks *different from* the way she looked on stage.

h. the **reason** is **that** . . ., *not* the **reason** is **because** . . .

POOR: The *reason* we allow boat people is *because* we believe in human rights.
BETTER: The *reason* we allow boat people is *that* we believe in human rights.

3. Prepositions may be used at the end of a sentence when any change of position would be awkward.

AWKWARD: They are friends with whom it is worthwhile to talk.
BETTER: They are friends worth talking *to*.

AWKWARD: For what are you charging me?
BETTER: What are you charging me *for?*

4. Distinguish between a preposition and a conjunction.

a. **like** is a preposition (introduces a *phrase*)
as, as if, as though are conjunctions (introduce *clauses*)

RIGHT: It looks *like* rain.
      phrase

RIGHT: It looks *as if* it will rain.
      clause

b. **without** is a preposition
unless is a conjunction

RIGHT: You can't make bricks *without* straw.
RIGHT: You can't succeed *unless* you try.

WRONG: I cannot do the work *without* you help me.
RIGHT: I cannot do the work *unless* you help me.

5. Avoid barbarisms! Choose the right word.

WRONG: *Among* you and *I*, this car rides better.
RIGHT: *Between* you and *me*, this car rides better.

WRONG: *Being that* he is older, he has senior privileges.
RIGHT: *Since* he is older, he has senior privileges.

WRONG: Let's wait *on she* and her sister to come.
RIGHT: Let's wait *for her* and her sister to come.

Exercise—Prepositions and Conjunctions

Choose the correct expression in parentheses.

1. The nurse took the bandage (off, off of) my finger.
2. Why are you still angry (at, with) me?
3. (For whom, Whom) are you looking for?
4. Be careful when stepping off a curb (among, between) two cars.
5. The little child stood fidgeting (beside, besides) his mother.
6. You could (of, have) heard a pin drop.
7. They must (of, have) known that you were listening.
8. We should (have, of) given some kind of warning.
9. A fox walked right (in, into) the trap we set for it.
10. A teenager tries to look different (than, from) adults.
11. Between you and (I, me), what is all the fuss about?
12. She gets a larger allowance (being that, because) she is older.
13. The city cannot support the poor (without, unless) the Federal Government provides special funds.
14. He fell in love with a blonde princess just (like, as) they do in storybooks.
15. (Since, Being as) the sales tax has increased, the price of goods has also gone up.
16. Tell me what you need (beside, besides) pencils.
17. All the members of the Student Council were waiting (on, for) a decision by the principal.
18. I had to borrow a dollar (from, off) my friend.
19. They left the party (along about, about) ten o'clock.
20. Our garage is located (near, near to) the kitchen.

Review of Prepositions and Conjunctions

A. Supply the information required to complete the statements below.

1. Two kinds of connecting words used in tying together the ideas of a sentence are __?__ and __?__.
2. Besides linking groups of words together grammatically, these connectives also serve to show the __?__ between them.
3. A word used to connect a noun or a pronoun with some other word in the sentence is called a __?__.
4. A preposition serves to show *direction*, or __?__, or __?__ in a sentence.
5. By idiomatic use of prepositions we mean that certain verbs require certain prepositions:
   a. to fall in love __?__ someone
   b. to pay attention __?__ the speaker
   c. to adapt a story __?__ the screen
   d. to differ __?__ another in appearance
   e. to argue __?__ a person about a topic
6. A word used to connect words, phrases, or clauses is called a __?__.
7. Two kinds of conjunctions are (*a*) __?__, which connects two main clauses; and (*b*) __?__, which joins a main clause with a dependent clause.
8. A subordinate conjunction shows the relation between ideas expressed according to *time*, __?__, __?__, or __?__.

B. Errors to avoid in using prepositions and conjunctions are of several types. Rewrite the sentences below.

1. *unnecessary prepositions:*
   For whom do you want a piece of cake for?
2. *confusion between prepositions:*
   Colonial homes are different than Japanese dwellings.
3. *confusion between prepositions and conjunctions:*
   You can't make an omelette without you break the eggs.
4. *barbarisms or non-accepted usage:*
   Being as you are so nice, you may have more candy.

C. Write the correct connective in each of the following sentences. Can you give the reason for your choice?

1. Is the atmosphere on the moon different (from, than) the atmosphere here on earth?

2. If creatures really live there, will they be monsters or ordinary folk (like, as) we are?
3. (Being that, Since) the expedition discovered rocks and minerals on the planet, every nation claims possession.
4. (Without, Unless) you have some scientific training, you will have to depend on your imagination to understand this.
5. When school ends, the youngsters fly out (like, as if) they were the cork popping out of a bottle.
6. Sometimes the reason the audience laughs is (that, because) the studio crew on TV holds up a "laugh" card.
7. Why is the referee so angry (with, at) the players?
8. Put the ball (among, between) the two painted white lines.
9. She quietly sat down (besides, beside) her boyfriend.
10. Someone must (have, of) turned on the automatic sprinkler.
11. Save your pennies and watch them grow (in, into) dollars.
12. The monitor collected all the papers (off of, off) the desks.
13. Share the work (among, between) all the workers.
14. She could (have, of) finished the job in half the time.
15. The happiest family consists (in, of) happy individuals.
16. All folk songs sound (like, as if) they come from the heart.
17. Last summer, Lewis earned (like, about) two hundred dollars.
18. Please tell me where you (live, live at) during the winter.
19. You cannot vote (except, unless) you are over eighteen.
20. Some persons can play the piano (as though, like) they have a natural ear for music.
21. We entertained the Smiths (to, at) dinner last evening.
22. Did her testimony agree (with, to) the facts presented in court?
23. The audience gasped when the acrobats swung (off of, off) the high trapeze in the circus act.
24. The reason I came back is (because, that) I needed money.
25. We waited but it wasn't long (when, before) the mail arrived.
26. A quartz watch is quite different (from, than) a timepiece with a stem wind.
27. Mildred decided to name her son Jack, (for, from) his uncle.
28. The lawyer asked whether she agreed (with, in) the judge's decision.
29. You will not get better (unless, without) you follow the doctor's orders.
30. Dr. Bella is well liked (between, among) his co-workers at the medical laboratory.

Chapter 11

Interjections

Up with people! We are made of flesh and blood and nerves. When we feel happy, we smile; when we feel sad, we cry. We are humans, alive with power to show joy, grief, anger, disgust, fear, envy, surprise, yearning, etc. We are not statues of stone, but creatures moved by events and people. This is true all over the world.

Friendly Eskimos rub noses in greeting, while we shake hands and say *Hello!* The excited Spaniards watching a bullfight will shout a rousing *Ole!* or *Caramba!* Italians enjoying a beautifully sung aria will exclaim *Bravo!* or *Viva!* The French call for a star to appear again by shouting *Encore!* or *Bis!* In America, our rock and roll enthusiasts scream at the band leader *One more time!* Or if disappointed, they *Boo!* These are all interjections used to show how people feel.

DEFINITION OF INTERJECTION

An *interjection* is a word or phrase used to show strong or sudden feeling. It usually expresses surprise, approval, or disapproval.

The word *interjection* comes from the Latin *inter* meaning "between"; *ject* meaning "to throw"; and *ion* meaning "the act of." Therefore, an interjection is a word or phrase thrown into a sentence.

Although the interjection has no grammatical connection with the sentence, it does have a very close connection with the meaning because the interjection sets forth the emotion or mood of the speaker or writer.

CAPITALIZING AND PUNCTUATING INTERJECTIONS

In *speaking*, a powerful emotion may be shown by the person's tone, gesture, dramatic posture, etc. Thumbs down means "no." Thumbs up means "yes." Applause shows approval. Stamping of feet shows impatience.

In *writing*, the clues to an emotion are provided by certain capitalization and punctuation signals.

Capital letters show strong emotion:

> *Alas!* We shall never see her again.
> *What a pity!* The whale population is decreasing rapidly.

Small letters show mild feeling:

> We are young and, *oh,* so glad.
> To you this is nothing, but, *ah,* what a difference to me.

Exclamation points show strong emotion:

> "*Bah! humbug!*" growled Scrooge at his nephew.
> "*No! Never!*" swore the tortured spy.

Commas show mild feeling:

> But, *gosh,* what are we going to do now?
> Oh, *shucks,* I forgot my umbrella again.

Caution: Don't overdo the use of the interjection. It is a kind of childish exaggeration to make everything appear stirring and important, even though it might be only a trifling matter. You probably have noticed how the comics overuse interjections such as *zam! zowie! zounds! oof! pow! bam! brrr! crash!*

LIST OF INTERJECTIONS

Oh!	Well!	Of course!	Ole!
Ah!	Watch it!	Congratulations!	Encore!
Hurrah!	Bah!	Oh my gosh!	Viva!
Alas!	Great!	For goodness sake!	Boo!
Look out!	At last!	Hi-ho!	Shucks!
Aha!	Great Scott!	Hello, there!	Bravo!

Exercises—Interjections

A. Using appropriate capitalization and punctuation, rewrite these expressions correctly as part of complete statements.

EXAMPLE:
liberty equality fraternity or death
The battle cry of the French Republic was "Liberty, equality, fraternity —or death!"

1. down with tyrants
2. freedom now
3. thanks a lot
4. danger curve ahead
5. slow down toll booth ahead
6. in this corner the world's champion
7. last call all aboard
8. for shame
9. good gracious
10. such nonsense

B. Write ten original statements using the list of interjections given on the previous page.

Exercise—Expressing the Mood or Feeling

Write complete statements expressing the mood or feeling suggested by the words given below.

	MOOD	WORD
1.	approval	Bravo!
2.	surprise	Really!
3.	disgust	Bah!
4.	amusement	Aha!
5.	anger	Stop it!
6.	disbelief	Bosh!
7.	joy	Cheers!
8.	pity	Alas!
9.	pleasure	Welcome!
10.	anxiety	Where oh where!
11.	disapproval	Not on your life!
12.	alarm	Watch out!
13.	grief	So sorry!
14.	weariness	At last!
15.	ridicule	Says who!
16.	cordiality	A toast!
17.	scolding	Nonsense!
18.	attention-getting	Quiet!
19.	request	Please!
20.	surrender	All right!

Review of Interjections

A. Complete these statements correctly.

1. To show strong or sudden feeling, you may use an __?__.
2. When speaking, a powerful emotion may be shown by a person's tone or __?__.
3. When writing, the clues to the emotion are provided by __?__ and __?__ signals.
4. A capital letter and an __?__ are used to show __?__ emotion or deep feeling.
5. A small letter and a __?__ are used to show __?__ emotion or less feeling.
6. Internationally recognized expressions of approval for a fine performance include the Spanish __?__, the Italian __?__, and the French __?__.

B. Find interjections to match each of the emotions or moods. Write sentences using them.

1. surprise	6. ridicule
2. joy	7. attention-getting
3. disbelief	8. disapproval
4. sorrow	9. weariness
5. approval	10. scolding

C. Rewrite the following passage with special attention to the appropriate capitalization and punctuation required to show emotion or emphasis. At the same time, notice the slanting lines that divide the thoughts into sentences.

A CLOSE CALL

Well we were driving a rented car along a narrow winding road in the mountains / / caution blind curve ahead said a sign / / a truck came barreling downhill/ /hey look where you're going the driver shouted/ /holy smoke cried Myles/ /there's no place to go/ /his brakes screeched the wheels to a stop/ / the truck came charging like a monster while the onlookers gestured excitedly/ /crunch the mudguard ripped across our fender/ /thank goodness nobody got hurt/ / oh boy that was a close call/ /

Chapter 12

Spell Common Words Accurately

WHY IS SPELLING IMPORTANT?

There was a time in the history of this country when the ability to spell was considered the badge of education and the sign of intelligence. Children and grown-ups used to travel many miles by horse and buggy or on foot to attend a spelling bee in the village schoolhouse. The two teams would line up to face each other publicly with the same rivalry and interest that today we find devoted to baseball. This famous indoor sport—the spelling bee—has been revived, and schoolrooms once again buzz with the excitement of an old-fashioned bee. The notable difference, however, lies in the fact that the present-day lists do not consist of "hard words" selected from an arbitrary list of lengthy strangers. Classes today struggle for mastery of the familiar demons like *separate*, *occasionally*, and *foreigner*.

Everybody realizes that the ability to spell correctly the words that are used most often in friendly notes and in business letters is an absolute necessity. For an error in spelling is the sort of glaring mistake which makes us blush and may cause us to lose social prestige. In school, these misspellings lower ratings on examinations in every subject. Outside of school, misspellings not only embarrass the writer but may lead to tragic blunders. For example, if the commanding officer orders *billets* for a group of soldiers, and a careless secretary writes the order as *bullets*, instead of receiving food and lodging some unlucky persons might face the firing squad. Watch your step, please!

SELF-CHECKING QUIZ IN SPELLING

A. Rewrite these words supplying *ei* or *ie*.

1. handkerch_?_?_f
2. rec_?_?_ve
3. for_?_?_gner
4. anc_?_?_nt
5. n_?_?_ghbor
6. n_?_?_ther
7. bel_?_?_ve
8. c_?_?_ling
9. w_?_?_ght
10. l_?_?_sure

B. Some of these words drop the final *e* before a suffix beginning with a vowel. Be careful of those that keep the *e*.

1. prepare + ing = __?__
2. desire + able = __?__
3. courage + ous = __?__
4. approve + al = __?__
5. love + ing = __?__

6. notice + able = __?__
7. reduce + ible = __?__
8. promise + ing = __?__
9. argue + ed = __?__
10. change + able = __?__

C. Some of these words drop the final *e* before a suffix beginning with a consonant. Others keep the *e*.

1. hope + less = __?__
2. life + like = __?__
3. nine + teen = __?__
4. awe + ful = __?__
5. due + ly = __?__

6. safe + ty = __?__
7. whole + some = __?__
8. move + ment = __?__
9. wise + dom = __?__
10. sincere + ly = __?__

D. Be careful when adding a prefix to a word. Which ones have double letters? Watch your step!

1. dis + appoint = __?__
2. dis + satisfied = __?__
3. dis + appear = __?__
4. dis + solve = __?__
5. mis + spelled = __?__

6. un + natural = __?__
7. un + necessary = __?__
8. un + afraid = __?__
9. mis + statement = __?__
10. mis + take = __?__

ANSWERS

A.
1. handkerchief
2. receive
3. foreigner
4. ancient
5. neighbor
6. neither
7. believe
8. ceiling
9. weight
10. leisure

B.
1. preparing
2. desirable
3. courageous
4. approval
5. loving
6. noticeable
7. reducible
8. promising
9. argued
10. changeable

C.
1. hopeless
2. lifelike
3. nineteen
4. awful
5. duly
6. safety
7. wholesome
8. movement
9. wisdom
10. sincerely

D. 1. disappoint
   2. dissatisfied
   3. disappear
   4. dissolve
   5. misspelled
   6. unnatural
   7. unnecessary
   8. unafraid
   9. misstatement
   10. mistake

WHY IS ENGLISH SPELLING DIFFICULT?

1. *We do not have a single letter to represent a single sound.*

   Here's an old puzzle: "How do you spell FISH?" The answer is *ghoti* because:

   > *gh* represents F in cough
   > *o*　represents I in women
   > *ti* represents SH in nation

2. *We have silent letters that we spell out in writing words.*

   > *p* and *e* are silent in *p*neumonia
   > *e* and *g* are silent in for*eig*n
   > *w* and *t* are silent in w*res*tling

3. *There are many pairs of words that sound alike but are spelled differently.*

aloud, allowed	piece, peace
stake, steak	coarse, course

THE MAIN CAUSES FOR MAKING SPELLING ERRORS

Some pupils are born good spellers. Most of us have to learn to be very careful about spelling. Be honest with yourself in figuring out your own personal weakness. Here is a little quiz to help you discover the main causes for spelling blunders.

1. *Seeing the word as it is actually written.*
   Do you notice that *chocolate* has an *o* before the *l?*

2. *Speaking with careful pronunciation of sounds.*
   Do you say *Febuary* instead of *February?*

3. *Listening with attention to catch the right sounds.*
   Do you hear *umberella* instead of *umbrella?*

4. *Reading without skipping over some letters.*
   Do you read *libary* instead of *library?*

5. *Separating the parts of a word to see the combination.*
   Do you see *keen ness* or *kee ness? book keeper* or *boo keeper?*

FIVE STEPS TO IMPROVE YOUR SPELLING

1. Look carefully at the word.	accidentally
2. Pronounce it correctly.	ˌak-sə-'dent-lē
3. Tell what it means.	happening by chance
4. Spell it orally.	a-c-c-i-d-e-n-t-a-l-l-y
5. Write it from memory.	accidentally

SOME IMPORTANT SPELLING RULES

1. Drop the final *e* when adding *ing*.

   love, loving   desire, desiring

   Spell these words correctly.

   move   + ing   tease   + ing
   write + ing   care   + ing

2. Drop the final *e* when adding *able*, but retain the final *e* when adding *able* to words ending in *ce* or *ge*.

   love, lovable   service, serviceable
   use, usable   change, changeable

   endure + able   notice   + able
   move   + able   manage + able

3. Change *y* to *i* when adding a syllable beginning with a consonant.

   lazy, lazily, laziness   easy, easily, easiness

   angry + ly   happy + ness
   busy + ly   ready + ness

4. When a word of one syllable ends in a single consonant preceded by a single vowel, double the final consonant before adding *ing* or *ed*.

   step, stepping, stepped   chop, chopping, chopped

   stop   + ed   let   + ing
   chat   + ed   hit   + ing

5. Double the final consonant in words of two syllables when the last syllable is accented and you are adding an ending beginning with a vowel.

occur	+ ed = occurred		forget	+ ing = forgetting
transfer	+ ed = transferred		prefer	+ ing = preferring

permit	+ ed	forgot	+ en
prefer	+ ed	occur	+ ing

6. Place *i* before *e*, except after *c*, or when sounded like *a* as in "neighbor" and "weigh."

IE	CEI		EI
believe	receive	neither	either
achieve	deceive	seize	weird
grief	conceive	leisure	neighbor
relief	perceive	weight	freight
thieves	receipt	feign	foreign
sieve	ceiling	beige	sleigh
quiet	deceit	reign	eight
friend	conceit	veil	vein

Exercise—Spelling Rules

Below you are given a complete word and a suffix. Combine the two into one correctly spelled word. In some instances, however, you are to rewrite a word by supplying either ei or ie.

1. stir + *ing*	18. occur + *ed*	35. swim + *ing*
2. argue + *able*	19. rel_?_?_f	36. bel_?_?_ve
3. lovely + *ness*	20. regret + *ing*	37. begin + *ing*
4. th_?_?_f	21. happy + *ly*	38. drop + *ed*
5. get + *ing*	22. grab + *ing*	39. for_?_?_gn
6. admire + *able*	23. value + *able*	40. desire + *able*
7. dine + *ing*	24. change + *ing*	41. rec_?_?_pt
8. commit + *ed*	25. heavy + *ly*	42. change + *able*
9. come + *ing*	26. knowledge + *able*	43. skid + *ed*
10. busy + *ly*	27. fr_?_?_nd	44. sense + *ing*
11. sit + *ing*	28. fit + *ed*	45. refer + *ed*
12. slam + *ed*	29. transfer + *ing*	46. lose + *ing*
13. peace + *able*	30. write + *ing*	47. submit + *ed*
14. rec_?_?_ve	31. steady + *ness*	48. bel_?_?_f
15. love + *ing*	32. qu_?_?_t	49. lazy + *ly*
16. lucky + *ly*	33. save + *ing*	50. n_?_?_ghbor
17. service + *able*	34. trace + *able*	

SPELLING LIST

Which words occur frequently enough in the affairs of the home, the school, the shop, and the office to merit serious study? Everyone should compose a list as the need arises. An individual spelling list kept in alphabetical order may serve as a handy guide whenever the writer wishes to check his or her work. The following list contains a useful series of words chosen widely from the most common activities people engage in. Since it is arranged in alphabetical order, it will not only provide much material for the purpose of study and testing, but will also serve as a valuable reference list during the writing of letters and compositions. Of course, a knowledge of the meaning of the words should go together with a knowledge of the spelling.

A
ability
absence
abstract
academy
accept
accident
account
accurate
ache
acid
acknowledge
acquaintance
acquire
action
activity
actual
actually
addition
additional
administrator
admission
adopt
advancement
advantage
advertised
affair
against
agency
agent
agreeable

agreement
agriculture
airplane
aisle
algebra
already
although
altogether
ambition
ambitious
ambulance
amendment
American
amount
ample
analyze
animal
announce
annual
annually
answer
answering
anxious
anybody
apologize
appearance
apply
approve
arithmetic
arouse
arrival

arrived
arrow
article
artificial
assign
associate
association
assume
assurance
astonish
athlete
athletic
Atlantic
attached
attain
attempt
attendance
attitude
audience
auditor
August
author
automobile
autumn
avenue
average
aviator

B
baggage
balloon

ballot
banana
bandage
banquet
basement
bathe
bathing
battery
battle
beast
beautiful
before
beggar
beginning
behave
behavior
believe
belong
beneath
benefit
bicycle
biggest
birth
biscuit
blanket
blizzard
blossom
bonus
booklet
booth
bought

boundary
bouquet
bracelet
brake
bravery
breathe
brief
British
bruise
bucket
building
bullet
bulletin
burden
bureau
business
busy
butter
button

C
cabbage
calendar
campaign
canal
cancel
capacity
career
careful
carefully
carnival

carpenter
carriage
cartoon
caution
cedar
celebrate
celery
cellar
cement
certain
certainly
certificate
chairperson
chapel
character
chauffeur
chimney
chocolate
choice
choose
chopping
chosen
Christian
church
circle
citizen
civics
client
closing
cloth
clothe
clothing
coarse
coffee
collection
college
colonies
colony
column
comfort
coming
commerce
committee
community
companies

company
compare
complete
completely
composition
concern
concerning
concert
conclude
conclusion
confer
confirm
congress
considerable
constantly
constitution
continue
convenience
conversation
cooperative
copies
cordial
cordially
corporation
corrected
correspond
country
coupon
courage
courteous
cousin
covering
crash
crawl
culture
cupboard
curious
current
cushion
custom
customer

D

daily
data

decide
decision
declaration
defeat
defend
definite
definitely
degree
delayed
delicate
delicious
delivery
department
dependent
deposit
describe
description
desert
design
desire
dessert
devoted
dictionary
difficult
difficulty
digging
diploma
disappoint
discount
discourage
discover
discussion
disease
disguise
disgusted
disposal
dissatisfied
dissatisfy
distinguish
divide
double
drama
drawing
dressing
drift

driving
dropped
due
duplicate
durable

E

earnest
easily
educate
education
efficient
eighteen
either
election
electric
electrical
electricity
elm
elsewhere
emergency
employer
employment
emptied
empty
encourage
endurance
enemies
energy
engaged
engine
engineer
English
enormous
enrolled
enter
entertain
entertainment
enthusiasm
entirely
entrance
equality
equally
equipment
equipped

eraser
errand
especially
establish
esteemed
estimate
evergreen
evidently
exact
exactly
examination
examine
excellence
excellent
except
exception
exceptional
exchange
excite
exciting
excuse
executive
exercise
exhaust
exhibit
exhibition
expected
expense
expensive
expire
explain
explaining
explanation
explore
extremely

F

fabric
factor
failure
faithful
familiar
family
famous
fanned

farming	geography	honest	internal	leisure
fasten	geometry	honesty	international	lengthen
father	geranium	honorable	interrupt	liable
favorable	germ	hope	introduction	librarian
favorite	glasses	hoping	invent	library
February	golf	however	invention	lightning
federal	govern	humor	investigate	limp
fender	government	hungry	investment	liquid
ferry	gradually	hurriedly	invoice	literary
festival	graduate	hygiene	involved	literature
fierce	graduating	hymn	irrigate	loan
figuring	grammar	hyphen	irrigation	lonesome
finally	grateful		item	lose
financial	gratitude	**I**		losing
fire fighter	greeting		**J**	lucky
foliage	grocery	identify		luncheon
football	guardian	illustrate	janitor	
forced	guide	imagine	jealous	**M**
foreign	guilt	immediately	jewel	
forest	guilty	immense	jewelry	machine
formerly	gymnasium	import	journal	machinery
formula		impression	journey	magazine
fortunate	**H**	improvement	journeys	maintain
fortune		improving	judge	majority
forty	hail	increase	July	management
foul	hammer	independence	junior	manager
foundation	handkerchief	indicate	justice	manner
fountain	happiness	individual	justify	manual
fourteen	happy	industry		manufacture
freight	harbor	information	**K**	marched
French	haste	injury	keeping	material
friend	hastily	inquiry	kettle	meadow
friendship	hatch	insect	kindergarten	meant
frighten	headache	inside	knee	meantime
fundamental	health	inspect	knives	mechanical
furnace	healthy	inspector	knob	medicine
furnish	heavy	instance	knot	membership
furniture	height	instead	knowledge	merchandise
further	helped	institution		merchant
	hereafter	instruction	**L**	merely
G	hereby	instructor	label	merit
	hero	insurance	ladies	message
garage	hesitate	intention	language	metal
generous	hire	interest	laundry	meter
gentlemen	history	interesting	league	method
genuine	holding	interfere	legislature	mineral

mining
minute
mischief
missed
misspell
moderate
moisture
mountain
museum
musical

N

national
natural
naturally
nature
necessary
necessity
necktie
neglect
neither
nephew
nervous
nevertheless
newspaper
nickel
niece
nineteen
ninety
ninth
normal
northern
notice
notified
notify
November
numerous

O

obedience
obedient
objection
obligation
obliged
occasion

occasionally
occupant
occupy
occurred
ocean
October
official
often
onion
opera
operate
operating
opportunity
opposite
orchard
ordinary
organize
original
originally
orphan
ostrich
overcoat
oyster

P

package
parade
parallel
pardon
park
particular
partner
payment
peculiar
pencil
people
permanent
permission
personal
physical
physician
pickle
pierce
plane

plank
planned
planning
pleasant
pleasure
poison
police officer
policy
political
popular
population
possess
possession
potatoes
praise
prayer
precious
prefer
premium
prepaid
preparing
preposition
present
president
prettiest
previous
primary
principal
principle
privilege
probably
proceed
process
procure
profession
professional
profit
promote
prompt
proof
prosperity
providing
publish
publisher
punish

Q

qualities
quality
quantity
quarrel
quarter
questions
quite
quotation
quoted

R

radio
raise
rapidly
reaching
readily
realizing
really
rebel
receipt
receive
reception
recess
recommend
referred
referring
refreshment
refused
regardless
register
regular
regularly
regulation
relations
relative
relief
relieve
religion
remainder
remedy
remember
removed
renter

replying
representative
requested
residence
resign
resource
respect
respectfully
retreat
revolutionary
rhubarb
riding
roof

S

sacrifice
safely
safety
sailor
salad
salary
salesperson
samples
sandwich
sanitary
satisfactory
satisfy
Saturday
savage
scarcely
scarcity
scatter
scenery
schedule
scholar
science
scientific
screen
search
secretary
seize
seldom
selfish
seller
senate

senior	squirrel	teacher	Tuesday	volunteer
sense	standard	tease	tunnel	voting
separate	starch	telegram	twenty	voyage
September	starve	telegraph	twice	
series	statue	telephone	type	**W**
serious	stomach	temperature		wait
service	stopped	tennis	**U**	wasteful
session	straight	terrible	umpire	weather
seventy	strength	territory	unfortunate	Wednesday
shadow	strenuous	testimony	uniform	weight
shave	studied	Thanksgiving	union	welcome
shoulder	studying	themselves	university	welfare
siege	succeed	thereafter	until	wharf
sigh	success	therefore	unusual	whenever
signature	suggest	thirsty	urge	whether
silence	suitable	thirteen	useful	which
similar	Sunday	thorough	using	whip
sincere	sunshine	thoroughly	usually	whisper
sincerely	superinten-	Thursday		women
sister	dent	timid	**V**	wondering
slice	supervisor	tobacco	vacant	workshop
slippery	suppose	tongue	valuable	worry
snowed	surface	tooth	variety	worse
social	surgeon	total	various	wrap
society	surgery	touch	vegetable	wreck
soldier	surplus	tractor	vicinity	wrist
soliciting	surrender	traffic	victory	writer
solo	swamp	transporta-	village	
somewhat	sympathy	tion	violin	**Y**
special		trimmed	vision	
spending	**T**	troop	visited	yeast
spiritual	talent	truly	voice	yesterday
splendid	tariff	truth	volume	yourselves

Exercises—Spelling

A. Write the word, correctly spelled, that completes each of the following sentences.

1. You may write with either a pen or a pe__?__l.
2. The day after Tuesday is We__?__y.
3. A sa__?__r is a member of the U.S. Navy.
4. In order to become a teacher, you must be a c__?__e graduate.
5. You will find many interesting books in your school li__?__y.

6. One who trains for a sport such as boxing, baseball, swimming, running, etc., is called an at__?__e.
7. Who is the prime minister of the Br__?__h government?
8. Another name for a five-cent coin is a ni__?__.
9. My youngest brother is now attending ki__?__n; next year he will enter the first grade of elementary school.
10. Another name for a pilot of airplanes is an av__?__r.
11. Robert Louis Stevenson is the au__?__r of the book *Treasure Island*.
12. Camels can be found in the Sahara De__?__t, a barren region in Africa.
13. Henry had a cough, so Dr. Smith gave him some med__?__ to drink three times a day.
14. A diamond is a very precious je__?__l.
15. The number that follows 89 is ni__?__y.
16. The head of a school is a prin__?__.
17. Fe__?__y is the second month of the year.
18. You rub out a mistake with an er__?__r.
19. One consults a ca__?__r to determine dates.
20. The number that follows 39 is fo__?__y.
21. When in doubt about the spelling of a word, consult a di__?__y.
22. Go to the store and buy some oranges, apples, pears, peaches, ba__?__s.
23. The verb to ba__?__ means "to wash yourself," as in a tub of water.
24. One who begs for money is a be__?__r.
25. The word *bike* is the shortened name for a bi__?__e.
26. A bunch of flowers is also called a bo__?__t of flowers.
27. A person who earns a living by driving an automobile is a ch__?__r.
28. Ar__?__c, the science of numbers and figures, is a subject everyone must study in elementary school.
29. To drive a nail into a piece of wood, we use a tool called a ha__?__r.
30. We should always sneeze and cough into our ha__?__f, so as not to spread germs.
31. America won its in__?__ce in 1776, an event we celebrate on the Fourth of July.
32. The plural of *knife* is kn__?__s.
33. Joe, your trousers are too short; ask your mother to len__?__n them.
34. Washington was the first pr__?__t of our country.
35. Up the tree jumped the frightened sq__?__l.
36. Whenever John writes me, he closes his letter, "Si__?__y yours."
37. We shall have pie a la mode for de__?__t tonight.
38. With my steak I would like to have French fried po__?__s.

39. Co__?__e is America's popular beverage, especially at breakfast time.
40. The number which follows seventeen is e__?__n.

B. Write the misspelled word or words in each group correctly.

1. lose, Saturday simpathy, urge
2. cancel, occassion, electrick, knee
3. civics, accept, daily, meret
4. jewal, article, healthy, ampel
5. drift, beggar, relief, victry
6. civics, untill, oporate, height
7. circle, type, definit, ache
8. banana, useing, finally, really
9. suceed, library, ment, delivery
10. financial, nephew, truely, educate
11. quarral, Wednesday, soldier, due
12. atheletic, drama, artical, poison
13. germ, excellent, actual, preceed
14. adopt, British, goverment, punish
15. assign, fabric, talant, heroe
16. nickle, church, ocupy, inside
17. academy, certin, popular, collige
18. August, erasor, whip, proceed
19. whether, totil, guilt, univercity
20. decide, beleive, pensil, October
21. seventy, driveing, yesterday, answer
22. finaly, eighteen, relief, famous
23. soldier, canal, circal, comeing
24. dissapoint, twice, defeat, justise
25. wreck, English, aviater, knifes
26. hastyly, northen, nineth, cancel
27. knee, baggige, violin, relitive
28. silense, height, imense, until
29. interfear, using, vision, delivary
30. fender, wisper, probibly, bruise
31. normil, vacant, teaze, golf
32. unusual, originaly, timid, opera
33. mountin, prompt, harbor, arrivil
34. famous, friendship, seenery, attemt
35. sanitary, bonus, volume, surfice
36. inseckt, telegram, readyly, errand
37. civics, safly, agency, booklit
38. endurince, degree, maintain, familiar
39. colony, corrispond, excelent, examine
40. traffick, fasten, assureance, design
41. imagin, territory, preposition, coffe
42. perminent, already, previous, telephone
43. exciteing, diploma, seperate, cellar
44. screen, admission, regular, accidant
45. exercise, machinary, beautifull, declaration
46. chairperson, nephew, carefuly, campain
47. definit, insted, disguise, French
48. February, anser, lunchin, primary
49. balloon, honorable, mispell, handkerchief
50. ninth, messige, chimney, ocurred

Chapter 13

Prefixes and Suffixes

PREFIXES AND SUFFIXES FOR SPELLING AND WORD BUILDING

A valuable way of enlarging your vocabulary is to pay attention to those powerful little syllables called *prefixes* and *suffixes*. They are powerful because you can change the meaning of a word by simply attaching them to the beginning or the ending. They work as surely as the switches on a railroad track in sending a train either straight ahead or in another direction. Make these prefixes and suffixes part of your active working vocabulary, and you will be surprised to see how you can change your stock of words from insufficient to sufficient, or from unsatisfactory to satisfactory. Notice how *in* ("not") and *un* ("not") switched the meaning of *sufficient* and *satisfactory* in the previous sentence. Be an engineer with words. Get into the driver's seat and learn to recognize the signals all along the track.

Another important use of prefixes and suffixes is the forming of parts of speech. For example, by adding *ation*, you change the verb *decorate* into the noun *decoration*. And you can form new words, too. For example, to describe a bus that runs between cities, you use the prefix *inter* (meaning "between") to form the word *intercity*.

Exercises—Prefixes and Suffixes

A. Prefixes meaning "not" or "the opposite" are these: *un, im, in, il, ir, dis,* and *mis.* Change the meaning of each of the words below to the exact opposite meaning by adding a prefix. Examples:

> happy, *un*happy   legal, *il*legal
> perfect, *im*perfect   regular, *ir*regular
> active, *in*active   please, *dis*please
>   direct, *mis*direct

1. continue	6. expert	11. understand	16. possible
2. important	7. observant	12. pure	17. definite
3. real	8. calculate	13. capable	18. agreeable
4. logical	9. allow	14. legible	19. prove
5. appear	10. responsible	15. probable	20. necessary

B. Change each of the following words below to mean "a person" or "one who" by adding *er* or *or* and making any necessary change in spelling. Examples:

buy, buy*er*   act, act*or*
play, play*er*   sail, sail*or*

1. sell	6. announce	11. profess	16. build
2. rent	7. teach	12. govern	17. orate
3. instruct	8. edit	13. export	18. supervise
4. advise	9. speak	14. inspect	19. clean
5. win	10. senate	15. manage	20. operate

C. Change each of the following words below to mean "a person" or "one who" by adding *ist* or *ian*, making any necessary change in spelling. Examples:

science, scient*ist*   history, histor*ian*

1. grammar	6. violin	11. colony	16. humor
2. special	7. military	12. mathematics	17. guard
3. piano	8. pharmacy	13. electric	18. humanity
4. art	9. pacify	14. machine	19. biology
5. library	10. music	15. magic	20. journal

D. To change adjectives into adverbs, add *ly* to each of the following words, making any necessary change in spelling. Examples:

final, final*ly*   hasty, hasti*ly*
disastrous, disastrous*ly*

1. admirable	6. necessary	11. sturdy	16. frequent
2. lazy	7. mischievous	12. nice	17. sincere
3. entire	8. careful	13. crazy	18. happy
4. careless	9. sure	14. sorrowful	19. definite
5. easy	10. satisfactory	15. considerable	20. disagreeable

E. To change verbs into nouns, add *ance* or *ence* to the words below, making any necessary change in spelling. Examples:

assist, assist*ance*   refer, refer*ence*
remember, remembr*ance*   reside, resid*ence*

1. perform	6. correspond	11. attend	16. observe
2. acquaint	7. abound	12. accept	17. confer
3. allow	8. endure	13. continue	18. insure
4. repent	9. occur	14. depend	19. appear
5. persevere	10. guide	15. prefer	20. excel

F. To change verbs into nouns or adjectives, add *ant* or *ent* to the words below, making any necessary change in spelling. Examples:

assist, assist*ant*   reside, resid*ent*

1. attend	6. differ	11. correspond	16. consult
2. consist	7. defend	12. persist	17. resist
3. superintend	8. preside	13. observe	18. insist
4. import	9. repel	14. occupy	19. expect
5. serve	10. result	15. please	20. urge

PREFIXES FOR SPELLING AND WORD BUILDING

Prefixes **are syllables placed at the beginning of words to change or modify the words.**

	PREFIX	MEANING	WORDS
1.	ante	before	anteroom, antedate, antechamber
2.	anti	against	antibiotic, antislavery, antiwar
3.	bi	two	bicycle, biped, bifocal
4.	circum	around	circumference, circuit, circumnavigate
5.	dia	through	diameter, diathermy, diagonal
6.	dis	opposite	disagree, disappoint, dissolve
7.	ex	out	exclude, expel, exclaim
8.	fore	before	forehand, forecast, foretell
9.	in	not	invisible, inexcusable, inexperience
10.	inter	between	interrupt, interscholastic, interplay
11.	mis	wrong	misspell, misunderstand, mistake
12.	mono	one	monolog, monochrome, monotony
13.	post	after	postscript, postpone, postdate
14.	pre	before	prevent, predict, prescribe
15.	re	again	review, reminder, renew
16.	semi	half	semicircle, semiprecious, semiannual
17.	sub	under	submarine, subsoil, subnormal
18.	super	over	superhuman, superfine, superhighway
19.	trans	across	transoceanic, transport, transfusion
20.	un	not	unknown, unnoticed, unnatural

Exercise—Prefixes for Spelling and Word Building

Add the prefix to each word element below and spell the newly formed combination correctly. Find the meanings in the dictionary.

1. ante + cedent
   ante + nuptial
   ante + chamber

2. anti + dote
   anti + body
   anti + toxin

3. bi + monthly
   bi + racial
   bi + cameral

4. circum + stance
   circum + vent
   circum + scribe

5. dia + dem
   dia + gram
   dia + meter

6. dis + able
   dis + appear
   dis + card

7. ex + ceed
   ex + cept
   ex + change

8. fore + runner
   fore + arm
   fore + warn

9. in + capable
   in + definite
   in + convenient

10. inter + fere
    inter + national
    inter + ject

11. mis + inform
    mis + carry
    mis + shaped

12. mono + plane
    mono + rail
    mono + gram

13. post + payment
    post + graduate
    post + mortem

14. pre + view
    pre + historic
    pre + mature

15. re + cover
    re + enter
    re + turn

16. semi + colon
    semi + final
    semi + civilized

17. sub + conscious
    sub + due
    sub + standard

18. super + power
    super + heat
    super + vision

19. trans + action
    trans + form
    trans + plant

20. un + claimed
    un + doubted
    un + favorable

SUFFIXES FOR SPELLING AND WORD BUILDING

Suffixes **are word-endings used to form other words or different parts of speech.**

$$
\begin{array}{ll}
\text{sweet} + \text{ly} = \text{sweetly} & \text{(adjective to adverb)} \\
\text{sweet} + \text{ness} = \text{sweetness} & \text{(adjective to noun)}
\end{array}
$$

Sometimes the spelling of the original word changes before adding a suffix.

$$
\begin{array}{lll}
\text{force} & + \text{ible} = \text{forcible} & \text{(drop the } e\text{)} \\
\text{change} & + \text{ing} = \text{changing} & \text{(drop the } e\text{)} \\
\text{pretty} & + \text{ly} = \text{prettily} & \text{(change the } y \text{ to } i\text{)}
\end{array}
$$

	SUFFIX	MEANING	WORDS
1.	ance	state of being	attendance, appearance
2.	ary	place where	aviary, capillary
3.	able	capable of being	durable, perishable
4.	ation	action, condition	decoration, civilization
5.	cy	state of being	fancy, currency
6.	ence	state of being	confidence, excellence
7.	er	one who	speaker, dancer
8.	fy	to make	purify, terrify
9.	ible	capable of being	responsible, visible
10.	ice	quality, state	cowardice, justice
11.	ity	state of being	timidity, equality
12.	ly	manner, like	kindly, accidentally
13.	ment	condition, state	movement, nourishment
14.	or	one who	ancestor, orator
15.	ness	quality, state	goodness, gentleness
16.	some	pertaining to	handsome, wearisome
17.	ship	quality, state	friendship, hardship
18.	tude	state of being	gratitude, certitude
19.	ous	full of	courageous, precious
20.	ism	quality, state	idealism, mannerism

Exercise—Suffixes for Spelling and Word Building

Add the suffix to each word or word element and spell the newly formed word correctly. Find the meanings in the dictionary.

1. ambul + ance
   domin + ance
   inherit + ance

2. custom + ary
   dignit + ary
   ordin + ary

3. laugh + able
   punish + able
   desire + able

4. converse + ation
   declare + ation
   found + ation

5. dependence + cy
   militant + cy
   occupant + cy

6. reside + ence
   confer + ence
   refer + ence

7. perform + er
   interview + er
   wrestle + er

8. simple + fy
   glory + fy
   solid + fy

9. defense + ible
   reverse + ible
   comprehend + ible

10. serve + ice
    just + ice
    avar + ice

11. acid + ity
    calam + ity
    fratern + ity

12. unusual + ly
    beneficial + ly
    successful + ly

13. entangle + ment
    amaze + ment
    experi + ment

14. audit + or
    credit + or
    invent + or

15. clever + ness
    bashful + ness
    keen + ness

16. fear + some
    glad + some
    worry + some

17. companion + ship
    leader + ship
    partner + ship

18. forti + tude
    soli + tude
    apti + tude

19. glory + ous
    adventure + ous
    marvel + ous

20. critic + ism
    journal + ism
    vandal + ism

Chapter 14

Contractions

Contractions are shortened forms of words used chiefly in conversation and in friendly letters.

They indicate in writing the slurring which takes place naturally in speaking. Although they have a place in ordinary speaking and in letters to friends, they should never be used in business letters. Business letters require the full spelling of words because they are more formal in style.

An *apostrophe* must be inserted to show the omission of a letter or letters from the spelling of the word. For example:

INFORMAL: *You're* the one *they've* been looking for.
FORMAL: *You are* the one *they have* been looking for.

's for *is*

it's	it is
that's	that is
what's	what is
he's	he is
she's	she is
there's	there is
where's	where is
who's	who is

n't for *not*

aren't	are not	haven't	have not
can't	cannot	isn't	is not
didn't	did not	shouldn't	should not
doesn't	does not	wasn't	was not
don't	do not	weren't	were not
hadn't	had not	won't	will not
hasn't	has not	wouldn't	would not

'm for *am*

I'm	I am

've for *have*

I've	I have
we've	we have
you've	you have
they've	they have

'll for *will* or *shall*

you'll	you will or you shall
he'll	he will or he shall
she'll	she will or she shall
it'll	it will or it shall
they'll	they will or they shall
I'll	I will or I shall
we'll	we will or we shall

's for *us*

let's	let us

're for *are*

we're	we are
you're	you are
they're	they are

' for *v*

ne'er	never
o'er	over
e'er	ever

't for *it*

'tis	it is
'twas	it was

Exercises—Contractions

A. In each of the following sentences, write the word in parentheses that makes the sentence correct.

1. I hope she (doesn't, don't) blame me.
2. (It's, Its) a beautiful bird.
3. The dog ate (its, it's) meat.
4. (Thats, That's) not true.
5. They (don't, doesn't) like him.
6. (Who's, Whose) going to the game?
7. They (wasn't, weren't) here.
8. Why (don't, doesn't) he talk to you?
9. (Let's, Lets) go to the movies.
10. (It's, Its) wing is broken.
11. Mother says she (don't, doesn't) know the time.
12. I hope (its, it's) not too late.
13. (Who's, Whose) book did you borrow?
14. Gina said that they (weren't, wasn't) at home.
15. Do you doubt that (hes, he's) telling the truth?
16. Fanny wants to know (whose, who's) crying.
17. (Wheres, Where's) my blue and red sweater?
18. The dog barked at (its, it's) master.
19. (Lets, Let's) not ask Mother until tonight.
20. (Whose, Who's) raincoat are you wearing?

B. Write the contraction for each of the following.

1. I am	11. he is	21. would not	31. she is
2. who is	12. do not	22. they have	32. over
3. it is	13. we have	23. that is	33. is not
4. I have	14. she shall	24. had not	34. she will
5. were not	15. did not	25. I shall	35. there is
6. I will	16. they shall	26. where is	36. has not
7. are not	17. you will	27. should not	37. it will
8. cannot	18. we are	28. they will	38. we shall
9. you are	19. was not	29. will not	39. what is
10. have not	20. does not	30. he will	40. you have

Chapter 15

Abbreviations

Abbreviations are short cuts in the spelling of long names and technical terms.

They are useful forms to recognize, especially when consulting a reference book like the dictionary. Notice the period at the end of each abbreviation.

Terms Used in English and in Reference Books

abbr.	abbreviation	**p.p.**	past participle
adj.	adjective	**pers.**	person
adv.	adverb	**pl., plur.**	plural
ant.	antonym	**poss.**	possessive
conj.	conjunction	**prep.**	preposition
dict.	dictionary	**pr. p.**	present participle
fem.	feminine	**pron.**	pronoun; pronunciation
gen.	gender	**punct.**	punctuation
gram.	grammar	**r.o.**	run-on sentence
interj.	interjection	**s.s.**	sentence structure
masc.	masculine	**sing.**	singular
neg.	negative	**sp.**	spelling
nom.	nominative	**subj.**	subject
n.	noun	**suff.**	suffix
no.	number	**superl.**	superlative
obj.	objective	**syn.**	synonym
par.	paragraph	**vocab.**	vocabulary
part.	participle		

(*Note:* For simplicity, reference books may omit periods.)

Days of the Week

Mon.	Monday	**Fri.**	Friday
Tues.	Tuesday	**Sat.**	Saturday
Wed.	Wednesday	**Sun.**	Sunday
Thur., Thurs.	Thursday		

Months of the Year

Jan.	January	**Sept.**	September
Feb.	February	**Oct.**	October
Mar.	March	**Nov.**	November
Apr.	April	**Dec.**	December
Aug.	August		

(*Note:* May, June, and July are not abbreviated.)

The United States

The first column lists the standard abbreviations, and the second contains the "two-letter" abbreviations (no periods) requested by the U.S. Postal Service for use in addressing mail.

Ala.	**AL**	Alabama	**Mont.**	**MT**	Montana
Alas.	**AK**	Alaska	**Nebr.**	**NE**	Nebraska
Ariz.	**AZ**	Arizona	**Nev.**	**NV**	Nevada
Ark.	**AR**	Arkansas	**N. H.**	**NH**	New Hampshire
Calif.	**CA**	California	**N. J.**	**NJ**	New Jersey
Colo.	**CO**	Colorado	**N. Mex.**	**NM**	New Mexico
Conn.	**CT**	Connecticut	**N. Y.**	**NY**	New York
Del.	**DE**	Delaware	**N. C.**	**NC**	North Carolina
D.C.	**DC**	District of Columbia	**N. Dak.**	**ND**	North Dakota
Fla.	**FL**	Florida	**O.**	**OH**	Ohio
Ga.	**GA**	Georgia	**Okla.**	**OK**	Oklahoma
Haw.	**HI**	Hawaii	**Oreg.**	**OR**	Oregon
Ida.	**ID**	Idaho	**Pa.**	**PA**	Pennsylvania
Ill.	**IL**	Illinois	**R. I.**	**RI**	Rhode Island
Ind.	**IN**	Indiana	**S. C.**	**SC**	South Carolina
Ia.	**IA**	Iowa	**S. Dak.**	**SD**	South Dakota
Kans.	**KS**	Kansas	**Tenn.**	**TN**	Tennessee
Ky.	**KY**	Kentucky	**Tex.**	**TX**	Texas
La.	**LA**	Louisiana	**Ut.**	**UT**	Utah
Me.	**ME**	Maine	**Vt.**	**VT**	Vermont
Md.	**MD**	Maryland	**Va.**	**VA**	Virginia
Mass.	**MA**	Massachusetts	**Wash.**	**WA**	Washington
Mich.	**MI**	Michigan	**W. Va.**	**WV**	West Virginia
Minn.	**MN**	Minnesota	**Wis.**	**WI**	Wisconsin
Miss.	**MS**	Mississippi	**Wyo.**	**WY**	Wyoming
Mo.	**MO**	Missouri			

Miscellaneous

ad., advt.	advertisement	**Messrs.**	Gentlemen
a.m.	before noon	**mo.**	month
Am., Amer.	American	**m.o.**	money order
amt.	amount	**Mr.**	Mister, adult man
Ave.	Avenue	**Mrs.**	Mistress, married woman
bbl.	barrel	**Mt.**	Mount
bldg.	building	**N.**	North
Blvd.	Boulevard	**oz.**	ounce
Capt.	Captain	**p.**	page
cf.	compare	**p.m.**	after noon
chap.	chapter	**P.O.**	post office
Co.	Company, County	**pp.**	pages
c/o	care of	**Pres.**	President
C.O.D.	cash on delivery	**Prin.**	Principal
Col.	Colonel	**P.S.**	Public School
do.	the same (ditto)	**qt.**	quart
doz.	dozen	**Rd.**	Road
Dr.	Doctor	**ref.**	refer to
E.	East	**R.R.**	railroad
ea.	each	**Ry.**	railway
e.g.	for example	**S.**	South
etc.	and so forth	**Sr.**	Senior
ft.	foot, feet	**S.S.**	steamship
gal.	gallon	**St.**	Street
Gov.	Governor	**Supt.**	Superintendent
govt.	government	**tr.**	transfer
Hon.	Honorable	**TV**	television
H.S.	High School	**U.S.**	United States
ht.	height	**Vice-Pres.**	Vice-President
i.e.	that is	**V.I.P.**	very important person
in.	inch	**viz.**	namely
Jr.	Junior	**W.**	West
kg.	kilogram	**wk.**	week
km.	kilometer	**Xmas.**	Christmas
l.	liter	**yd.**	yard
Maj.	Major		

Exercises—Abbreviations

A. Write the word or expression for which each of the following abbreviations stands.

1. oz.	6. a.m.	11. no.	16. Jr.
2. mo.	7. n.	12. syn.	17. Mar.
3. Aug.	8. etc.	13. W. Va.	18. Prin.
4. Ave.	9. P.O.	14. bbl.	19. fem.
5. Ore.	10. Pa.	15. ht.	20. Ill.

B. Write the abbreviation for each of the following expressions.

1. November	11. preposition	21. namely
2. Georgia	12. Street	22. compare
3. money order	13. Monday	23. refer to
4. abbreviation	14. west	24. transfer
5. Wednesday	15. Road	25. very important person
6. subject	16. feet	26. liter
7. that is	17. December	27. kilogram
8. New Jersey	18. railroad	28. kilometer
9. quart	19. Florida	29. run-on sentence
10. doctor	20. singular	30. sentence structure

Review of Spelling

A. Complete the following spelling rules correctly:

1. Change *y* to *i* when adding a syllable beginning with a __?__.
   Example: easy + ness = __?__

2. When a word of one syllable ends in a single consonant preceded by a single vowel, __?__ the final consonant before adding *ing* or *ed*.
   Example: stop + ing = __?__

3. Drop the final *e* before adding *ing*.
   Example: wave + ing = __?__

4. Drop the final *e* when adding *able*, but keep the final *e* when adding *able* to words ending in __?__ or __?__.
   Examples: notice + able = __?__
   change + able = __?__

5. Double the final consonant in words of two syllables when the last syllable is accented and you add an ending beginning with a __?__.
   Example: occur + ence = __?__

6. Place *i* before *e*, except after *c*, or when sounded like *a* as in __?__ and __?__.
   Examples: bel__?__ve, sl__?__gh (bells)

B. In each of the following groups of words, only one of the words is misspelled. Rewrite it correctly.

1. doctor, lawyer, druggist, libarian
2. mispell, secondary, kindergarten, college
3. Tuesday, Wednesday, Thrusday, Saturday
4. daily, weekly, monthly, loseing
5. necessary, government, capillary, accessory
6. cafateria, villain, separate, altogether
7. spoonful, occasionaly, monkey, penny
8. succeed, recede, proceding, exceed
9. foreigner, liesure, weird, belief
10. happiest, dictionery, deferred, interpreted

C. Rewrite each word, supplying the missing letters.

1. def__?__nition
2. re__?__ommend
3. fug__?__tive
4. accident__?__ly
5. sep__?__rate

6. Yours tru__?__
7. Yours respect__?__ly
8. Sincere__?__ yours
9. Cordial__?__ yours
10. Faithful__?__ yours

11. The ac__?__ demic course gives basic training for college.
12. The commer__?__al course prepares you for the business world.
13. The technic__?__ course leads toward engineering.
14. The gener__?__ course provides fundamental schooling.
15. Victims of the earthquake needed rel__?__f from suffering.
16. Everybody should have a hobby for l__?__sure-time activity.
17. A thirteen-month calend__?__r has been proposed for the year.
18. Boston is the capit__?__l of Massachusetts.
19. The police nabbed the burgl__?__r in the act of stealing.
20. You are mature when you feel respons__?__ble for your actions.
21. He plan__?__ (expected) to go to Europe last year.
22. The celebration occur__?__ (took place) on the Fourth of July.
23. His friend was transfer__?__ (shifted) to another area.
24. Her mother credit__?__ (believed) her explanation readily.
25. The oak tree is shed__?__ (dropping) its leaves.

D. Ask someone to dictate these words to you. By the way, these are really not so easy as they look. *Take care!*

1. doesn't
2. won't (for "will not")
3. can't (for "cannot")
4. its (belonging to "it")
5. whose (belonging to "whom")
6. nineteen
7. truly
8. weight
9. height
10. dropped
11. stopped
12. until
13. piece (a chunk or portion)
14. peace (no fighting!)
15. course (subject for study)
16. coarse (rough)
17. awful
18. either
19. neither
20. ceiling

21. relief
22. society
23. writing
24. excel
25. accept
26. spoonful
27. careful
28. scribble
29. ache
30. career
31. cousin
32. daily
33. diary
34. famous
35. modern
36. heroes
37. label
38. nickel
39. pencil
40. really

E. Complete the following:

1. Syllables placed at the beginning of words are called __?__.

    Examples: un + important = __?__

    re + construct = __?__

    trans + continental = __?__

2. Endings that are used to form other parts of speech are called __?__.

    Examples: sure + ly = __?__
    (adj.)   (adv.)

    teach + er = __?__
    (v.)   (n.)

    advantage + ous = __?__
    (n.)   (adj.)

F. Complete the following:

1. __?__ are shortened forms of words.

    Examples: it's = __?__

    don't = __?__

2. Choose the word that makes the sentence correct.
    a. (Who's, Whose) calling, please?
    b. We hope he (don't, doesn't) arrive late.
    c. Jack, (let's, lets) go for a swim.
    d. Are you sure (shes, she's) home?
    e. (Their, They're) friendly!

G. Write the abbreviations.

1. Principal
2. January
3. Oklahoma
4. synonym
5. west
6. ditto

Chapter 16

Punctuation and Capitalization
Are Aids to Reading

Wherever you go—by car, by plane, by boat, or on foot—you find directional signs. Traffic signals tell the driver to stop on red or go on green. A plane follows the light beacon or radio beam to make a safe landing. A ship steers by floating buoys to find the deep channels in the bay. On foot, you cross at the corner to avoid jaywalking. In the same way, whenever you read printed material, you follow the punctuation marks and the capital letters as traffic signals to stop, look, and listen!

DEFINITION OF PUNCTUATION

Punctuation is the separation of words by marks to make the meaning clear to the reader.

The meaning of *punctus* in Latin is "point." In speaking, you use a pause for a comma and a full stop for a period. Other signals serve special purposes.

CHIEF PUNCTUATION MARKS

> END OF THE SENTENCE:
>   period, question mark, exclamation point
>
> INSIDE THE SENTENCE:
>   comma, colon, semicolon, dash, apostrophe, dots
>
> OTHER MARKS:
>   parentheses, brackets, quotation marks

DEFINITION OF CAPITALIZATION

A *capital letter* is used as the initial letter of the first word of a sentence and the first word of each line of poetry; proper nouns and proper adjectives; titles of honor; etc.

In Latin the word *caput* means "head," and therefore suggests important rank or position.

A b c d E

Capitals Suggest Important Rank or Position.

AIDS TO READING

We read with our eyes and with our mind. Our eyes carry the written message by means of word-symbols which our mind can interpret into ideas. The speed and accuracy of our mind in understanding printed matter depends in large part, therefore, on the ease and sureness with which our eyes transmit the word-symbols. To help increase clearness and to avoid confusion, certain marks have been established as signposts or signals to the reader of a written page.

Try reading a passage without punctuation and capitalization. Notice how awkward and unnecessarily bothersome such reading can be. Then compare the ease and sureness with which you can understand the same passage when it contains the helpful signals of punctuation and capitalization.

NOT PUNCTUATED NOR CAPITALIZED	PROPERLY PUNCTUATED AND CAPITALIZED
words are interesting because they reflect mans moods actions and desires in a whole series of picturesque phrases the victorious uss lexington aircraft carrier was dubbed queen of the flattops the lazy art of daydreaming became building castles in spain franklin d roosevelt defined the rights of all free people as the four freedoms russia struck back at the nazi invaders with a weapon called the scorched earth policy thus words provide not only a living record of human affairs but also a trip to new countries of the mind	Words are interesting because they reflect man's moods, actions, and desires in a whole series of picturesque phrases. The victorious U.S.S. *Lexington*, aircraft carrier, was dubbed "queen of the flattops." The lazy art of daydreaming became "building castles in Spain." Franklin D. Roosevelt defined the rights of all free people as "the four freedoms." Russia struck back at the Nazi invaders with a weapon called "the scorched earth policy." Thus, words provide not only a living record of human affairs, but also a trip to new countries of the mind.

QUIZ YOURSELF

Punctuate and capitalize these statements in a way that will make the meaning clear.

1. If youre thin dont eat fast
2. If youre fat dont eat fast
3. Tell her before it rains cats and dogs open the umbrella
4. Our plane landed animals in the jungle scattered at sight.
5. Egyptians buried everything money jewelry treasures untold

Compare your answers with these. Did you get 100%?

1. If you're thin, don't eat fast.
2. If you're fat, don't eat. Fast!
3. Tell her before it rains cats and dogs: "Open the umbrella!"
4. Our plane landed; animals in the jungle scattered at sight.
5. Egyptians buried everything: money, jewelry, treasures untold.

Chapter 17

Punctuation Rules

Use a Period

1. After declarative and imperative sentences:

    DECLARATIVE
    We are going.
    I will talk to Joe.

    IMPERATIVE
    Go quickly.
    Talk to him.

2. After abbreviations and initials:

    Mr. Mrs. Ms. a.m. p.m. Dr. A. J. Gates i.e. etc.

Use a Question Mark ?

3. After an interrogative sentence:

    Where is she?
    "How are you feeling?" he asked.

4. *Note:* Use the period, instead of a question mark, at the end of an *indirect* question.

    INDIRECT QUESTION: I would like to know when you will be home.
    DIRECT QUESTION: When will you be home?

Use an Exclamation Point !

5. At the end of a sentence expressing strong emotion:

    What a beautiful day!   Let him go, right now!

6. After a short interjection:

    Ah! There she is!   So what!   Oh! Forget it.

Use a Comma [,]

7. To separate a series of words. (*Note:* The comma before *and* or *or* may be omitted.)

> We bought candy, cake, ice cream, and soda.
> Do you prefer watermelon, cantaloupe, or honeydew?

8. To set off an appositive (a word-group that directly follows a noun and gives added information):

> Robert Simmons, *my friend and classmate*, is ill.

9. To set off a noun in direct address (the person spoken to):

> *Frank*, where were you?

10. To separate the clauses of a compound sentence:

> Robert went skating after school, and Helen went bowling with Ellen.

11. To set off an introductory phrase:

> In the afternoon, we resumed painting the kitchen.

12. After an introductory adverbial clause:

> If you want to play a game of checkers tonight, come to my house.

13. To denote separation in dates and addresses:

> April 19, 1975   Los Angeles, California
> Ida was born on January 1, 1971, in Detroit, Michigan.
> We lived in Dayton, Ohio, for ten years.

14. After the salutation and the complimentary closing of a friendly letter:

> Dear Ruth,   Your friend,   As ever,

Exercise—Punctuation

These sentences lack both end punctuation and inside punctuation. Rewrite each sentence, supplying the necessary marks.

1. I went to the library Tuesday Wednesday and Friday
2. While waiting for the bus with Mary we met Dr Shaw

3. How is your sister feeling Jane inquired
4. Hurray Here comes our train
5. Jimmy go to the store for a loaf of bread
6. For the children we bought some candy ice cream and soda
7. Can you name the five Great Lakes
8. Nellie Wallace a friend of mine went to Chicago Illinois last week
9. Antonia have you finished your homework
10. We were only five miles from home and low on gas but not a gas station was open at that late hour

Use a Colon

15. After the salutation of a business letter:

    Dear Mr. Brady: Dear Sir or Madam:
    Dear Mrs. Lewis: To Whom It May Concern:

16. To introduce a list, an illustration, or a statement:

    I serve as a hospital volunteer three times a week: Tuesday, Thursday, and Sunday.

17. To separate the figures denoting hours and minutes when expressing time:

    6:15 a.m.   8:30 p.m.   10:45

Use a Semicolon

18. To separate members of a compound sentence when no conjunction is expressed:

    You should not be in school with such a bad cold; you should be home in bed.
    Nursing requires patience; such care is priceless.

Use Quotation Marks

19. To enclose the direct words of the speaker.

    "You are right," Miss Jones replied.   He said, "Thank you."

20. Be careful of broken quotations. Notice the change in meaning!

> The lawyer said, "The witness is a liar!"
> "The lawyer," said the witness, "is a liar!"

21. To indicate titles of *individual* short stories, poems, magazine articles, essays, songs, one-act plays. When indicating the title of a *full-length* novel, or a *collection* of plays or poems, or the title of a newspaper or magazine, you may underline instead of using quotation marks.

	INDIVIDUAL TITLES	FULL-LENGTH BOOKS OR COLLECTIONS
STORY:	"The Gold Bug"	World's Greatest Short Stories
POEM:	"The First Snowfall"	The Viking Book of Poetry
SONG:	"Heart of My Heart"	Everybody's Favorite Songs
ARTICLE:	"Life on the Fiji Islands"	National Geographic Magazine

22. *Note:* In printing, italics are used in place of underlining. Solid capitals may also be used.

Use an Apostrophe

23. To indicate the omission of a letter or letters:

> won't, isn't, let's, don't, it's (meaning *it is*), o'clock

24. To form the possessive case of nouns and indefinite pronouns:

> Bob's father, Rosa's mother, Judy's car, women's votes
> everyone's favorite, somebody's hat, anyone's choice

25. *Caution:* Personal pronouns in the possessive case never take an apostrophe.

> CORRECT: its, hers, theirs, ours, yours
> EXAMPLE: What's *yours* now will someday be *hers*.

Use a Dash

26. To show an abrupt change of thought in a sentence:

> Relax and sit down, but—here comes our bus!

27. To emphasize a word or group of words by setting it off from the rest:

There is one thing I will not permit—lateness.
Give me the address—the full address—of the bookstore.

Use Dots

28. To show a trailing off in the thought:

There's always time and hope and ...

29. To show the omission of words, as in a quotation:

"Silently, one by one, ... blossomed the lovely stars."
(The three dots show the omission of the phrase "in the infinite meadows of heaven.")

Use Parentheses ( )

30. To set off explanatory material:

Smoking cigarettes may cause cancer (the deadliest disease) and shorten your life.

31. To write numbers in words, or to put words in numbers to show the correctness of figures.

Please find $20.00 (twenty dollars) enclosed.
Please find twenty dollars ($20.00) enclosed.

Use Brackets [ ]

32. To enclose comments, notes, or explanations which are written by someone else, *not* by the author or writer of the original text:

You have won the election. [Applause]

Exercise—Punctuation

These sentences lack both end punctuation and inside punctuation. Rewrite each sentence, supplying the necessary marks.

1. We left New York on August 4 1980 at 640 am
2. I have read the following books Robinson Crusoe Treasure Island and The Call of the Wild
3. When I called at his house to see him I was told he hadnt come home yet
4. There will be an assembly today at one oclock Mr Roberts announced
5. Miss Howard my teacher asked Do you expect to pass your examination
6. Mrs Franklin my brothers employer called at our house last night
7. At the theater the sign stated The show will start at three oclock
8. Although Mother was very angry with me she did not scold me but she insisted that I stay home Saturday to study for my exams
9. I bought the following newspapers the News the Monitor and the Times
10. Why didnt you visit Uncle Harry Dad asked
11. In Pride and Prejudice a novel by Jane Austen Mr Darcy was interested in Elizabeth the second Bennet daughter
12. Miss Williams asked Why dont you study more often
13. Lets buy a new color TV not too expensive of course for Mother on her birthday
14. Our new school building was completed March 1 1980 as scheduled
15. Whenever I meet Miss Burns she is well dressed she wears clothes very handsomely

CHANGING STYLES IN PUNCTUATION AND CAPITALIZATION

Some years ago the rule was, "When in doubt, punctuate." Thus, there was widespread use of commas wherever a pause occurred in a sentence. For example: "On a cold, dark, dull, dreary day in November, we wore warm, heavy, overcoats."

Today, since we're living in a computerized world with speed as our motto, the rule seems to be, "When in doubt, leave it out." Thus, we see no punctuation marks used by the computer in preparing statements and envelopes in business.

```
NORMAN SMITH
2270 NE 68 ST APT 923
FT LAUDERDALE FL 33308
```

Chapter 18

Capitalization Rules

USE CAPITAL LETTERS FOR

1. The first word of every sentence and the pronoun *I*.
   She and I are cousins.

2. The first word of every direct quotation:
   Byron wrote, "There is a pleasure in the pathless woods."

3. Proper nouns and proper adjectives:

New York—New Yorker	England—English
France—French	Spain—Spanish
Texas—Texan	California—Californian

4. The chief words in the title of a book, a newspaper, and a magazine, including the first word:
   I am reading "The Salamander," a good story.

5. Days of the week, months of the year, and holidays:
   Sunday, Monday, Tuesday, etc.
   January, February, March, etc.
   Labor Day, Columbus Day, Christmas, etc.
   Because of the Fourth of July, there was no school Monday.

6. *Note:* Do not capitalize the seasons of the year.
   spring, summer, autumn (fall), winter
   Most people take a summer vacation, but I prefer the winter.

7. Names referring to sacred writings or the Deity:
   the Bible, Old Testament, God, Jehovah, the Almighty, Psalms of David, the Ten Commandments

8. Titles of honor or office:
   Dad, Mother, Miss, Reverend, President, Senator, Mayor, Rabbi

9. Historical events, geographical places, important buildings, and sections of the country:
   the Battle of Bunker Hill, the Rocky Mountains, the White House, the East, the West, the North, the South

10. *Note:* When referring to direction, *north, south, east,* and *west* are not capitalized.

      My school is one mile north of Main Street.

Exercise—Capitalization

    In the following sentences, there are words that are not capitalized but should be. Write the words that should be capitalized.

1. Charles darwin, a scientist, exclaimed, "i do believe in god."
2. We received a letter from mother.
3. The mississippi river is the longest in the united states.
4. This bible was given to me by father kelly.
5. At this time of year, it is much warmer down south than out west.
6. According to the *new york times*, philadelphia is having its first snowstorm since thanksgiving.
7. How did you spend the fourth of july holiday, dr. thomas?
8. In the month of december, i was absent more often than in november or september.
9. The visiting days at brown hospital are monday, wednesday, friday, and sunday.
10. Father shouted, "who is playing the radio at this time of night?"
11. My english teacher is miss wilson.
12. The north is very cold in the month of december.
13. According to the *boston globe*, boston had more rain in may than in april.
14. President carter was succeeded by president reagan.
15. I am going to oak street to buy a magazine for mrs. lopez.
16. Have you ever seen the white house in washington, d.c.?
17. She said, "clara is a surgeon at hill street hospital."
18. My sister attends new york university, and my brother will enter dartmouth college in september.
19. Graduation exercises at city college are to be held on thursday.
20. Where are you going this labor day weekend, mr. barton?
21. My spanish teacher is miss johnson.
22. I met dad on main street.
23. I read of the chicago fire in the *evening journal*.
24. Henry was born in february, and harry was born in june.
25. Helen shouted, "your mother wants you immediately."
26. *The rime of the ancient mariner* is an enjoyable narrative poem.
27. We are going to aunt martha's house on sunday.
28. The adirondack mountains are very beautiful at this time of year.
29. Can you name two countries in central america?
30. Last summer debbie went to the middle east, and i went to puerto rico.

Exercises—Punctuation and Capitalization

A. Rewrite the following sentences so that each will be correct in punctuation and capitalization.

1. have you read the book *treasure island*
2. why dont you tell me what is wrong mother asked alice
3. we are going to cleveland ohio on thanskgiving day
4. i shall study french spanish or latin next term
5. louise received a new bible a deluxe edition for christmas
6. the convention was planned for september 15 1982 at 7 oclock
7. the rocket flight was postponed again it is now scheduled for tuesday
8. i have been to the catskill mountains the white mountains and lake george
9. she shouted who saw henry brown
10. this friday november 14 will be my birthday dad said
11. she replied lets go out for dinner and celebrate
12. everyone knows los angeles is not the capital of california
13. ann my sisters friend shouted be careful dont skate on thin ice
14. have you seen *david copperfield* the movie based on the novel by dickens
15. we are going to visit aunt martha this easter in her new home
16. louis is going south this winter he may go to miami beach florida
17. how are you feeling asked dr ruiz the optician
18. on thursday march 14 i am going to a surprise party
19. traffic laws were made for the protection of pedestrians and motorists and they must be obeyed by everyone
20. have you seen my sweater the blue one
21. i like both english and french but i dont like social studies
22. this sunday october 10 is our anniversary mother said
23. where are you going my father asked
24. frank why dont you write more carefully
25. ed received a watch a bike and roller skates for christmas
26. did you know that harrisburg is the capital of pennsylvania
27. this winter we are going to the west coast and honolulu hawaii
28. i dont know why shes crying dad replied
29. on tuesday he was in baltimore maryland and on wednesday in washington, dc
30. although i came home late from school today mother asked me to prepare dinner

B. Rewrite the following, dividing them into sentences and using correct punctuation and capitalization.

1. While i was walking along main street this afternoon i met dr garzone how are you albert he asked very well i replied
2. dr coryell our principal is well liked by everyone moreover she is probably the best teacher in our school dr coryell once said i hope i am helping to make you students good citizens
3. henry lewis my neighbor was hurt in an accident he was confined to grant hospital for four weeks last saturday february 18 he returned home always be careful while riding a bike at night he said to me when i visited him on sunday
4. i like english french and algebra i dont doubt that i will pass with high marks mother will be pleased i am sure always do your best she says
5. dr barrus announced there will be no school during the week commencing february 1 this action was taken as a means to conserve fuel he continued study hard during that week of idleness he said

Review of Punctuation and Capitalization

A. Supply the information needed to complete the statements below.

1. The word *punctuation* comes from the Latin word *punctus*, which means __?__ .
2. The separation of words by marks serves to make the __?__ clear to the reader.
3. The end of a sentence is shown by using one of these three marks: __?__ , __?__ , __?__ .
4. Inside a sentence, the chief punctuation marks are __?__ , __?__ , __?__ , __?__ , __?__ , __?__ .
5. Three other points or marks are: __?__ , __?__ , and __?__ .
6. To suggest important ideas, rank, or position, we use __?__ letters in spelling.
7. In the original Latin, the word *caput* means __?__ .
8. After declarative and imperative sentences, use the __?__ .
9. To separate a series of words, use the __?__ .
10. After the salutation of a friendly letter, use the __?__ .

11. After the salutation of a business letter, use the __?__ .
12. To separate members of a compound sentence when no conjunction is expressed, use the __?__ .
13. After an expression of strong emotion, use the __?__ .
14. To enclose the direct words of a speaker, use __?__ .
15. To form the possessive case of nouns, use the __?__ .
16. Personal pronouns in the possessive case never take the __?__ .
17. To show an abrupt change of thought in a sentence, use the __?__ .
18. To show a trailing off in the thought, use __?__ .
19. To set off explanatory material within a sentence, use __?__ .
20. To enclose comments, notes, or explanations, use __?__ .

B. Rewrite these sentences, inserting the proper punctuation and capitalization required to make the meaning clear and correct.

1. as hamlet lay dying his best friend said good night sweet prince
2. one of the most famous documents in american history is the bill of rights
3. great thinkers like socrates moses christ gandhi and others served as guides to humanity over the centuries
4. when the fair employment practices code became effective the minority groups in america got more jobs
5. to protect depositors in savings banks the federal deposit insurance corporation was formed
6. if you read the quotations on the new york stock exchange you will find that some prices go up while other prices go down
7. do you know the source of the saying a penny saved is a penny earned
8. the bible says blessed are the peacemakers for they shall be called the children of god
9. generations of immigrants have called america the land of opportunity and found happiness here
10. isnt all education designed to free us from ignorance fear superstition prejudice
11. someone upstairs must wonder when looking down at our rolling planet and watching our behavior whether perhaps
12. on new years day we make some resolutions but why dont we keep our promises
13. let us promise to begin not tomorrow but today to do our very best in all things
14. the track and cross-country team thats the sport to join viola suggested
15. as far as im concerned there are really only three sports i enjoy swimming golfing and walking are there any others that have a lifetime value
16. next sunday will be mothers day and next month fathers day and i wonder what gimmick will be next in the business world to capitalize on sentiment

17. alas the robins have fled from the trees because the neighbors got a vicious black cat and the laws of the jungle allow no mercy
18. shall i tell you how much ive hoped and prayed that youd be back home safe and sound my daughter
19. your honor we offer proof not suspicion that on the night of january 16 the defendant so help him god did wrongfully attack and seriously wound the complainant
20. why must all our days be spent in routine occupations when adventure calls secretly to the inner self where can you go to escape from it all

C. Rewrite this letter with the correct capitalization and punctuation. Getting a job requires 100% effort.

---

294 howard avenue
staten island new york 10301
may 28 19——

rural new yorker
333 west 30 street
new york new york 10001

dear sir

   i am applying for the position of clerical worker in your publishing office as advertised in the wall street journal yesterday here are my qualifications.

age	17 years
education	graduate of curtis high school where i successfully completed three years of mathematics two years of bookkeeping three years of social studies and four years of english
experience	worked for the past two years as clerk and secretary assisting mrs stone the head of the girls gym department
references	mrs w widdecombe 129 tysen place staten island new york 10301
	rev peter dolan st peters church st marks place staten island new york 10301

sincerely yours
joan k muller

Chapter 19

Vocabulary

HOW TO INCREASE YOUR COMMAND OF WORDS

Your vocabulary is the stock of words that you recognize and use. Building your vocabulary means developing your acquaintance with words not only in school but as a lifelong process of enrichment. Vocabulary building means finding different uses for old words and current uses for new terms. Swallowing the dictionary is not the answer; getting to know the resources of the dictionary provides a giant step in the right direction. Wide reading of books, newspapers, and magazines gives you a great leap forward. Experience is the greatest teacher because by experience you gain personal contact with things.

Studying this section will stimulate you to become a word detective, a treasure hunter, and a philologist ("lover of words"). Are you interested in getting better grades in school, landing a good job someday, and becoming a well-rounded person? Start now!

WHY ARE WORDS POWERFUL WAYS OF COMMUNICATION?

SOME USES OF WORDS	SOME EXAMPLES
1. *Bring people together:*	"Let's pray for world peace!"
2. *Sell goods:*	"Not the cheapest, but the best."
3. *Form opinions:*	"Should your parents know where you are going tonight?"
4. *Create new ideas:*	"Space shuttle"—a spacecraft serving as a platform for scientific research, etc.
5. *Make wars:*	"Give me liberty or give me death!"
6. *Label things:*	"Microwave"—ultrahigh frequency radio waves
7. *Win your heart:*	"My love is like a red, red rose."
8. *Recall history:*	"The pen is mightier than the sword."
9. *Give information:*	How to make a million dollars.
10. *Show intelligence:*	There is a warm current running from the Gulf of Mexico to Europe that influences the climate along the Eastern coast of the United States.

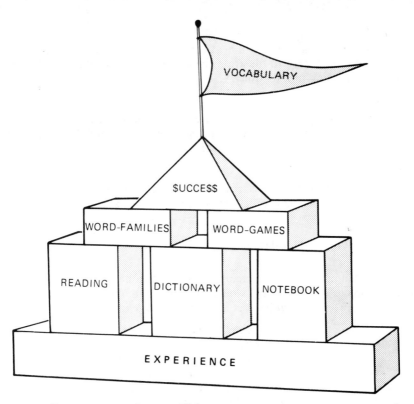

Use all six ways, and you will be on your way to greater success in school, on the job, and in your personal life.

SIX WAYS OF BUILDING YOUR VOCABULARY

1. Experience

Widen your range of experience by firsthand contact with people, events, community activities, church affairs, etc. Life is the greatest teacher of words and everything else.

2. Reading

Develop the habit of reading books, newspapers, and magazines based on your interests, hobbies, and intended vocation. Reading is one of the chief tools in broadening your background.

3. Dictionary

Get better acquainted with the contents and arrangement of words in the dictionary. The dictionary is a "must" for everyone. Keep one handy for ready reference at home or school.

4. Notebook

Collect words and keep a neat copy of new words in your notebook. Copy the phrase to illustrate the actual use of the new word. Check the meaning in a dictionary.

5. Word-Families

Study groups of words that are related in structure and meaning because of prefixes, roots, and suffixes. Latin and Greek parents have given us thousands of words.

6. Word-Games

Just for fun, become a crossword puzzle fan and solve other word games that appear in newspapers, magazines, and quiz books.

HOW LANGUAGE GROWS

A living language grows in many ways. English has become an international language by borrowing widely from other tongues to enrich its own vocabulary. From *French* have come rouge, garage, depot.

Italian:	camera, spaghetti, opera
Latin:	circus, scribble, credit
Greek:	meter, marathon, biology
Spanish:	guitar, armada, cigar
German:	waltz, beer, hamburger
Hebrew:	shalom, amen, sabbath
Celtic:	shamrock, blarney, whiskey

Other ways by which English has grown include shortening long words into words of one or two syllables, and combining two words into one.

fanatic	= fan	atomic bomb	= A-bomb
omnibus	= bus	Treasury bill	= T-bill
discothèque	= disco	nuclear plant	= nuke
gasoline	= gas	sky laboratory	= skylab
veterinary	= vet	situation comedy	= sitcom

Some words are formed from the first letters of other words. These are called *acronyms.*

TIP	= to insure promptness
AWACS	= Airborne Warning and Control System (planes)
UFO	= unidentified flying object

Newcomers in language may really be old-timers used in forming new expressions: *squawk box, hot rod, paperback, line dance, supermarket, moonscape, astronaut, microfilm, tape recorder,* etc.

Exercise—How Language Grows

Can you complete these statements? Check your answers with a dictionary.

1. *Petite* was borrowed from (French, Spanish, Italian). __?__
2. *Frankfurter* came from (Polish, German, Turkish). __?__
3. *Antipasto* came from (Portuguese, Russian, Italian). __?__
4. *Wampum, caucus,* and *papoose* came from (Eskimo, African, American Indian) __?__ languages.
5. *Gasohol* combines parts of the words *gasoline* and __?__.
6. *Show biz* was shortened from *show b__?__*.
7. *Golf pro* abbreviates *golf pro__?__*.
8. *Kayo* or *K.O.* in boxing refers to a __?__.
9. *NATO* for North Atlantic Treaty Organization is an example of the kind of word called an __?__.
10. __?__ is short for "correct, all right."

USING THE DICTIONARY

We usually go to the dictionary to find the spelling, the meaning, or the pronunciation of a word. Actually, a good dictionary contains an encyclopedia of worthwhile information. Keep your dictionary always handy on your desk for ready reference.

The latest unabridged edition of *Webster's Third New International Dictionary*, issued in 1961, contains 450,000 separate vocabulary entries. It may interest you to look up a short word, *set*, which has 143 different uses. This will show you how important it is for you to select the meaning that fits the sentence! Here are a few sample sentences using *set:*

She *set* the clock.

(*set* = "regulated")

He had a *set* of three cards: the ten, jack, and the queen of spades.

(*set* = "series")

The chicken *set* on the egg and hatched it.

(*set* = "brooded")

Exercise—Choose the Meaning to Fit the Sentence

Write the word in parentheses that matches the meaning of the italicized word in each of these sentences.

1. Our assemblies are conducted in a *dignified* (careless, mechanical, indifferent, mannerly) way once a week.
2. His *opponent* (stranger, companion, foe, friend) shook hands with him before entering the boxing ring.
3. The cry for personal rights sometimes shows only *meager* (slight, excessive, wild, honest) understanding of personal responsibilities.
4. Before we repaired the garage, the cinder blocks seemed *decrepit* (solid, worn-out, loose, cemented) from age and weather.
5. Your gift to charity should be made not from duty but from *generosity* (stinginess, security, liberality, neutrality).
6. If your composition appears *illegible* (ungrammatical, unreadable, misspelled, sloppy), your rating will be poor.
7. When the wandering tribes were freed from *bondage* (loan, bombardment, slavery, ransom), they thanked God.
8. Surgeons make sure they do not *sever* (knot, cut, misplace, damage) an artery during an operation.
9. An obedient student gets a good personality rating, whereas an *obstinate* (gentle, submissive, stubborn, yielding) pupil receives demerits.
10. In the long run, happiness depends on making a reasonable *compromise* (adjustment, surrender, victory, flattery).

WORD FAMILIES

Words are like people. **A *word family* is a group of words having the same parents.** These common ancestors are called ***roots***. They form the main line of meaning. The leaves and branches are called ***prefixes*** and ***suffixes***. (See pages 147–152 for a discussion of prefixes and suffixes.)

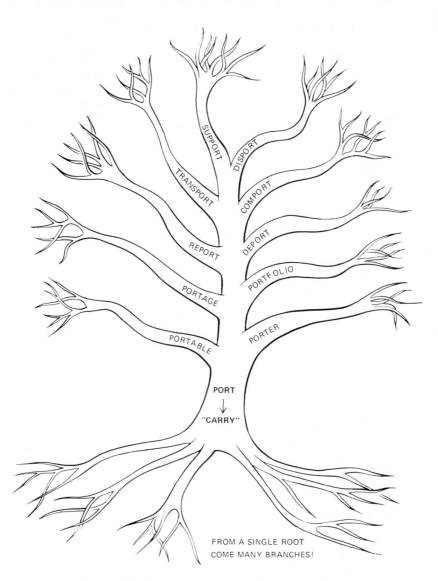

SUPPORT

DISPORT

TRANSPORT

COMPORT

REPORT

DEPORT

PORTAGE

PORTFOLIO

PORTABLE

PORTER

PORT
↓
"CARRY"

FROM A SINGLE ROOT
COME MANY BRANCHES!

porter, one who carries baggage
portable, able to be carried
portage, act of carrying
portfolio, a carrying case
transport, to carry across
import, to carry into

report, to carry back an account
comport, to carry oneself, to behave
deport, to carry away, to banish
disport, to carry away from work, to play
support, to carry the weight, to bear
export, to carry out of

BORROWINGS FROM LATIN AND GREEK

Most parent words (roots) come from Latin and Greek. They are called "fertile" because they have produced countless offspring in our language. Get acquainted with these word families and you will be better able to recognize the meanings of many related words. Here are some examples to study and learn.

- **SCRIBE:** *write* (Latin)
  scribble, *write* carelessly and hastily
  describe, *write* about something
  manuscript, *written* by hand

  RELATED WORDS: Find their meaning in the dictionary.
inscribe	scripture	transcribe
prescription	postscript	subscription

- **DICT:** *speak* or *say* (Latin)
  dictate, *speak* or *say* something to be taken down
  contradict, *say* the opposite of something
  predict, *say* that something will happen in the future

  RELATED WORDS:
dictionary	malediction	dictaphone
benediction	verdict	valedictory

- **DUCT:** *lead* (Latin)
  conductor, *leader* of the band
  abduct, *lead* away
  aqueduct, *leading* water through a large pipe

  RELATED WORDS:
ductless	introduce	deduct
viaduct	product	reduce

- **SPECT:** *look* or *see* (Latin)
  spectacle, an unusual *sight* or view
  inspector, somebody who *looks* carefully over something
  spectroscope, an optical instrument to *see* radiation or light

  RELATED WORDS:
spectator	respect	specter
spectacular	retrospect	speculate

- **VERT:** *turn* (Latin)

  vertigo, dizziness, a feeling that everything is *turning*
  extrovert, a person who *turns* his or her attention away from self
  revert, *turn* back to a former habit or belief, etc.

  RELATED WORDS:

vertical	divert	subversive
convert	introvert	invert

- **GRAPH:** *write* (Greek)

  graphite, black lead used for *writing* (in pencils)
  graphology, the study of hand*writing*
  monograph, a *written* account about a single topic

  RELATED WORDS:

graphic	biography	lithography
geography	autobiography	telegraph

- **OLOGY:** *science* or *study* (Greek)

  biology, *science* of living things
  psychology, *study* of human behavior
  meteorology, *science* of weather prediction

  RELATED WORDS:

cardiology	etymology	numerology
dermatology	histology	zoology

- **PHONE:** *sound* (Greek)

  phonograph, *sound* reproducing machine
  phonics, reading taught by the *sound* of words
  telephone, system for sending *sound* to a distant point

  RELATED WORDS:

megaphone	audiophone	hydrophone
microphone	dictaphone	xylophone

- **PHILOS:** *love* (Greek)

  philosopher, one who *loves* wisdom
  bibliophile, one who *loves* books
  philharmonic, one who *loves* music

  RELATED WORDS:

philatelist	philologist	Francophile
philanthropist	philander	Anglophile

- **CHRONO:** *time* (Greek)
  chronometer, *time*piece used aboard ships at sea
  anachronism, something placed out of its proper *time*
  chronicle, record of events in the order of *time*

RELATED WORDS:

chronic	chronograph	chronogram
chronology	chronoscope	synchronize

Exercise—Word Families

Using the words provided in this section dealing with Latin and Greek parents of English words, write the word that fits the meaning in each sentence. As a clue, you may refer to the words based on the parent word given in parentheses.

1. The doctor wrote a __?__ for medicine the patient was to take every day until he felt better. (*scribe*)
2. The boss tried to save time in preparing letters for the secretary to type, so he spoke into the __?__ machine. (*dict*)
3. A traffic engineer figured out a way of directing heavy trucks away from residential areas by means of a __?__. (*duct*)
4. As we grow older, we sometimes remember days gone by, and we take a a look in __?__ by browsing through picture albums. (*spect*)
5. To divide a number by any fraction, you must turn the fraction over, or __?__ it, and then multiply the number. (*vert*)
6. One kind of interesting reading is the true life story, or __?__, of a popular hero or heroine. (*graph*)
7. Recent attempts at conquering heart disease have led to the development of __?__, or the study of the function of the heart. (*ology*)
8. The referee announced his decision to the crowd through a __?__ that carried the sound of his voice to the grandstand. (*phone*)
9. Andrew Carnegie used some of his millions to help others and became known as a great __?__. (*philos*)
10. Arranging a series of events according to the time when they happened is called making a __?__ of the events. (*chrono*)

Exercise—More Word Families From Latin

Using a dictionary, find more English words that come from these parents (roots).

LATIN ROOTS	MEANING	ENGLISH WORDS RELATED IN MEANING
1. cad, cas	fall	**cadence,** *fall* of voice in speaking, or *fall* of sound in music **cascade,** water*fall*
2. cede, cess	go	**recede,** *go* backward **process,** *go* forward toward some end or purpose
3. cide, cise	kill, cut	**germicide,** germ *killer* **incision,** *cut* into something
4. cur, course	run	**current,** *running* tide **discourse,** *running* talk
5. fact, fice	make, do	**factory,** place where things are *made* **orifice,** an opening *made,* such as a mouth
6. fer	carry	**refer,** *carry* something back to its source **transfer,** *carry* something across to another place
7. fide	trust	**fidelity,** *trust* or faithfulness **confide,** show *trust* by telling someone a secret
8. ject	throw	**project,** *throw* an image on a screen **inject,** *throw* or put into the body with a needle
9. jud, just	law, right	**judge,** one who administers the *law* **justice,** equal *rights* for all
10. junct	join	**junction,** place where two roads meet or *join* **conjunction,** a word which connects or *joins* other words
11. luc, lum	light	**lucid,** shining with *light* **illuminate,** *light*up
12. mand	order	**mandate,** an *order* by a court or nation **command,** an *order* by someone in authority

13. mis, mit	send	**mission,** group of persons *sent* for politics, business, religion
		permit, let something be *sent* through
14. ped	foot	**pedal,** a lever worked by the *foot*
		pedestrian, a traveler on *foot*
15. pend	hang	**pendulum,** a *hanging* device that swings in a clock
		pendant, a *hanging* ornament, as a necklace
16. pone, pose	put, place	**postpone,** *put* off to a later time
		position, *place*
17. rupt	break	**rupture,** *break*
		interrupt, *break* into, as in a conversation
18. sta	stand	**stationary,** *standing* still
		stable, *standing* securely
19. tact, tang	touch	**contact,** *touch* or meet
		tangible, capable of being *touched*
20. term	end	**terminal,** the *end,* as of a bus line or railroad
		determine, to set limits or bring to an *end*
21. tract	draw	**tractor,** vehicle used for *drawing* or hauling
		protractor, instrument for *drawing* angles on paper
22. vene, vent	come	**convene,** to *come* together in a group
		prevent, to keep from *coming* or happening
23. vict	win,	**victor,** person who *wins* or overcomes the opponent
	overcome	**convict,** person who was *overcome* by proof of guilt
24. voc	call	**vocation,** a *calling* to a particular occupation
		vocalist, a *caller* or singer
25. volve	roll	**revolver,** pistol with a turning or *rolling* cylinder of bullets
		involve, to *roll* with or take part in, as a discussion or problem

Exercise—More Word Families From Greek

Using a standard dictionary, find more English words derived from these original roots or parents.

GREEK ROOTS	MEANING	ENGLISH WORDS RELATED IN MEANING
1. anthropo	man	**anthropology,** the science of *man*, or of human beings **anther,** the *male* portion of a flower
2. astron	star	**astronomy,** the study of *stars* **astronaut,** a traveler in space moving toward the *stars*
3. auto	self	**autobiography,** the story of one's life written by one*self* **automobile,** a *self*-moving vehicle
4. bio	life	**biology,** the study of *life* **antibiotic,** a substance to destroy *life*
5. deca	ten	**decade,** *ten* years **decalogue,** *ten* commandments
6. demo	people	**democracy,** government by the *people* **epidemic,** widespread among *people*
7. geo	earth	**geology,** study of the formation of the *earth* **geography,** science of the *earth* and its inhabitants
8. hydro	water	**hydrogen,** with oxygen, a *water* former **hydroplane,** a craft that flies over *water*
9. logo	word	**dialog(ue),** exchange of *words* between people **theologian,** student of the *word* of God
10. metron	measure	**metronome,** instrument for *measuring* time in music **barometer,** instrument for *measuring* pressure in the atmosphere
11. mono	one, alone	**monolog(ue),** speech made by *one* person **monotone,** *one* sound
12. nomy	law, science	**economy,** *laws* of supply and demand **astronomy,** *science* of the stars

13. ortho	right	**orthodox,** *right* belief **orthodontal,** *right* or straightened position of teeth
14. pod	foot	**podiatrist,** *foot* specialist **chiropodist,** one who treats *foot* ailments
15. poly	many	**polyester,** *many* elements in a chemical compound **polychrome,** *many* colors
16. scope	see	**microscope,** instrument used to *see* minute objects **periscope,** instrument used to *see* while a submarine is underwater
17. tele	far	**telegraph,** apparatus for sending messages at a distance *far* off **telephone,** apparatus for speaking with someone *far* away
18. therm	heat	**thermometer,** device to measure *heat* or temperature of a person or of the atmosphere **thermal,** pertaining to *heat*
19. tri	three	**triangle,** a figure containing *three* angles **tripod,** a *three*-legged stand for a camera
20. zoon	animal	**zoology,** study of *animals* **protozoa,** one-celled *animal*

WHAT KINDS OF WORDS SHOULD YOU LEARN?

There are generally two large groups of words that belong to you: (1) your *speaking* vocabulary of bread-and-butter words used every day; and (2) your *reading* vocabulary of bookish words and phrases that you can recognize or identify. Obviously, your everyday word stock consists chiefly of expressions dealing with practical experience, human interest, and opinions about common matters. On the other hand, your reserve word-supply consists mainly of literary references, more polished journalistic phrases, and standard words used by educated persons. You need to widen your acquaintance with both kinds of vocabulary in order to gain surer command of expression. The art of writing and skill in everyday talk depend on your word power. Just take, for example, the different ways of saying something about a common thing.

Short, speaking words:	"cash on hand" or "dollars"
Slang, picturesque style:	"lettuce" or "greenbacks" or "bread"
Long, reading words:	"financial condition" (used by banks or businesses)
Literary quotation:	"The love of money is the root of all evil." (from the Bible)
Foreign borrowing:	"pecuniary affairs" (Latin *pecunia* = "money; originally property in cattle or sheep")

Thus, you can see money referred to as bills, coins, lettuce, sheep, or whatever people use. Remember some Native American tribes used beads or wampum as a means of exchange.

WORDS HAVE PERSONALITIES

Words *mean* something, but they may also *suggest* something because words have acquired personalities full of color, size, shape, and other qualities. Thus, every word carries more than a dictionary definition. It brings with it the variety of feelings that human beings share. For example, "Happy birthday!" carries memories of friends, presents, a party, etc. Specialists who handle words as a way of advertising goods or molding opinion are keenly aware of the flavor and power of words. *What kinds of words do you like? dislike?*

TALL WORDS?
skyscraper, television, astronaut, rocketry, pagoda

SHORT WORDS?
pin, dot, fur, sand, yes

SAD WORDS?
lost, failed, broken, forgotten, regret

SWEET WORDS?
perfume, starlight, music, honey, sunshine

HARD WORDS?
rock, knife, helmet, fist, jaw

SOFT WORDS?
cream, silk, cotton, sofa, feathers

CHOOSING THE RIGHT WORD

What are the levels of usage? Just as you wear ordinary clothes to a back-yard barbecue but dress up for a dinner party, you use words that fit the occasion. The two levels of usage are called:

- *Literary:* the formal, rather bookish style used in compositions and business letters
- *Conversational:* the informal, friendly style of plain talk used in telephoning or in face-to-face conversing

Of course, you realize that the right word is the one that best suits the time, place, and person. Some examples follow.

LITERARY LEVEL	CONVERSATIONAL LEVEL
1. may I inform you	let me tell you
2. no refund available	no money returned
3. balance due	pay the full amount now
4. delayed by traffic conditions	late because of the bus tie-up
5. prompt and punctual	right on time
6. elderly retired	senior citizens
7. avoid littering the area	drop it in the basket
8. no trespassing allowed	keep out
9. interpersonal relationships	getting along with others
10. the generation gap	the failure of teenagers and adults to understand each other

Exercise—Literary Level

Give the ordinary conversational way of expressing these ideas which are stated on a literary level.

1. Labor to keep alive in your breast that little spark of celestial fire—conscience. (George Washington)
2. My heart is like a singing bird. (Christina G. Rossetti)
3. Knowledge comes, but wisdom lingers. (Alfred, Lord Tennyson)
4. Joy lights the candles in my heart
   When you come in. (Babette Deutsch)
5. None but the brave deserves the fair. (John Dryden)

Exercise—Conversational Level

Using Bartlett's *Familiar Quotations*, Barbara Rowe's *The Book of Quotes*, or any other reference book, find the literary way of expressing these ideas which are stated in a conversational way. The author's name appears in parentheses.

1. Youth becomes romantic in spring. (Alfred, Lord Tennyson)
2. Great men inspire us to live better. (Henry Wadsworth Longfellow)
3. If you have belief in yourself, you will obtain what you aim for. (Kathryn Kuhlman)
4. A good book will last a long time. (John Milton)
5. Enjoy life because time marches on. (Robert Herrick)

WHAT IS "GOOD ENGLISH"?

Good English is the kind that is accepted and understood all over the world. It is the spoken or written language used in business, school, church, politics, TV programs, stage plays, books, newspapers, magazines, etc. This is called *Standard English.* Some examples follow:

> Enclosed find a check for ten dollars.
> Love thy neighbor.
> Vote for the right candidate.
> We now bring you tomorrow's weather forecast.
> Poetry is the rhythmical creation of beauty.

Nonstandard English refers to the kind of language limited to certain areas or occupations and is often illiterate. It may be found in some comics or heard in street talk. Regional speech and occupational slang have local acceptance, but good English will help your choice of job and your future anywhere.

> He almost blew it.
> Can you dig it?
> What a palooka he turned out to be!
> We hired a Gal Friday for the office on spec.
> She couldn't cut the mustard.

Good English is the badge of culture recognized everywhere.

HOW TO AVOID FAULTY DICTION

By *faulty diction* is meant the wrong use of words. You must use words according to their recognized meaning. Since popular usage at times confuses one word with another, it is your task to learn and use the correct words to express your ideas.

Sometimes a single error in diction can result in a serious social blunder. For example, if you respond to an invitation to a party with "I *except* your invitation" instead of writing "I *accept* your invitation," you are really saying just the opposite of what you wish! *Except* means "omit, or leave out"; *accept* means "agree to, or receive with approval." Therefore, be very careful to choose your words to express your ideas according to the recognized meaning of words in standard English.

ACCEPT—EXCEPT

Accept means "agree to, or receive with approval."
   I am happy to *accept* your offer to go to the dance.
Except means "omit, or leave out."
   For tomorrow, do exercise A *except* question 4.

ALREADY—ALL READY

Already means "by a particular time, or beforehand."
   He has *already* completed his homework.
All ready is a phrase of two words meaning "everyone was prepared."
   They were *all ready* to go home when they discovered that there was still more work to be done.

ALRIGHT—ALL RIGHT

Alright is not accepted in standard English and should be omitted from your writing.
All right is a phrase of two words meaning "satisfactory."
   That new suit is *all right* (not *alright*).

ALTOGETHER—ALL TOGETHER

Altogether means "entirely, or completely."
   The detective's solution to the crime was *altogether* right.
All together is a phrase of two words meaning "all in one place, or all in company."
   They decided to go to the dance *all together*.

AMONG—BETWEEN

Among refers to more than two persons or things.
My coat was *among* all the other missing items.

Between refers to only two persons or things.
The money was divided *between* Joan and me.

BESIDE-BESIDES

Beside means "near, close to."
Place your chair *beside* my desk.

Besides means "in addition to, moreover."
There are two in my family *besides* me.

BRING—TAKE

Bring suggests motion toward a speaker.
Bring the letter to me.

Take suggests motion away from a speaker.
Take the letter to the post office.

CAN—MAY

Can denotes power or ability.
Do you believe she *can* do the job?

May denotes permission.
May I speak with you?

DIFFERENT FROM—DIFFERENT THAN

Different should never be completed by *than* or *to* but always by *from*.
This pen is *different from* (not *different than*) any other.
Watercolor painting is *different from* (not *different to*) oil painting.

DON'T—DOESN'T

Don't means "do not."
Why *don't* they ask you?

Doesn't means "does not."
The pencil *doesn't* write.

INJURE—DAMAGE

Injure means "to harm someone."
Two persons were *injured* during the storm.

Damage means "to mar or break property."
The tornado *damaged* several buildings.

Learn the Basic Rules 195

Since *kind* and *sort* are singular in form, the proper way to use them is with singular modifiers. Therefore, in showing a personal preference or pointing out a particular type of thing, always say *this kind, that kind, this sort, that sort.*

Incorrect: My parents prefer *these kind of movies.*
Correct: My parents prefer *this kind of movie.*

Incorrect: I like *those sort of books.*
Correct: I like *that sort of book.*

LEARN—TEACH

Learn means "to acquire knowledge."
I should like to *learn* to swim.

Teach means "to give instruction."
I will *teach* you to skate."

LEAVE—LET

Leave means "to depart from."
You may *leave* the building.

Let means "to allow, to permit."
Let him go home.

OF—HAVE

Do not use *of* for *have.*
I *should have* (not *should of*) done my homework.

PARTY—PERSON

Party is used only in legal papers for "individual."
The *party* herein mentioned is responsible.

Person is the correct ordinary way of referring to "anybody."
Persons caught shoplifting will be prosecuted.

THERE—THEIR—THEY'RE

I looked *there* but didn't find it.   (adverb of location)
My brothers sold *their* boat.   (possessive pronoun)
They're buying a sports car.   (contraction of verb)

Don't confuse these three words.

We walked *to* (in the direction of) school.	(preposition)
The trunk was *too* (very) heavy to carry.	(adverb)
There are *two* (a couple of) men waiting to see you.	(adjective)

TRY AND—TRY TO

The correct form is *try to*.
Will you *try to* (not *try and*) come?

UNNECESSARY WORDS

Omit unnecessary or useless words, as the italicized words in the following sentences:

My brother *he* joined the Navy.
That *there* pen is hers.
This *here* pencil is mine.
Where is she *at?*
Take it off *of* the desk.
They *had* ought to go.
What kind of *a* pencil is it?

Exercise—Faulty Diction

Some of the sentences are incorrect and some are correct. Rewrite only those sentences that are incorrect.

1. My partner she isn't here today.
2. Why don't she do her homework?
3. The bus had ought to be here by now.
4. I cannot go with you, although I'd like too.
5. Between the three sweaters, I find it difficult to choose the one I like best.
6. This bike is different than the one I ordered.
7. I looked their for the timetable.
8. That kind of watch may be injured by overwinding.
9. I will try and go to the museum with you on Saturday.
10. That there man is my father.
11. We were already to go when it started to rain.
12. May she go to the carnival with me?
13. She said she would learn us the rules.
14. This here town is so small, it is not even on a map.
15. The tacos were divided between the five of us.
16. Put the chairs neatly beside the table.

17. Bring the money to the bank.
18. For tomorrow do all accept the sixth question.
19. I'm tired of trying to learn you to speak correctly.
20. Doesn't she remember who I am?
21. There are too more at home besides me.
22. He should of asked his parents first.
23. This here party is my homeroom teacher.
24. They offered a reward for the return of there lost dog.
25. Why don't she help you do the dishes?
26. Let us go to the beach altogether.
27. Leave the team go out and practice.
28. Put the radio on the table besides my bed.
29. The pen it doesn't write well.
30. Where is she staying at?
31. We walked to and from the store.
32. In appearance, she's very different than her sister.
33. Take the skirt to John, and he will shorten it.
34. Please try and be quiet.
35. She is injuring two many books with graffiti.
36. That there coat is nice looking.
37. Can I go shopping with you?
38. I'm supposed to buy these sort of paints.
39. Leave the magazine on my desk when you leave.
40. Just between the three of us, I don't like her.
41. I should of mailed the letter today.
42. The dog don't bark much.
43. Your mother she can sew well.
44. Angela's poster is not very different to mine.
45. I will learn you how to make a rag doll.
46. Sally doesn't live their.
47. Jane will try and do her homework before dinner.
48. Mary, where are you living at now?
49. She don't know how to develop her composition topic.
50. I should not have gone skating myself.
51. The girls in the next room are too noisy.
52. Is this floral arrangement alright?
53. Why don't the parrot keep still?
54. Where did Carmela say she would be at?
55. This here book is written in French.
56. Bring back the shopping cart to the store, Pat.
57. I'm trying to teach him to bake a cake.
58. She shouldn't have taken it off of the mantel.
59. My brother he thinks he's smart.
60. We should of won the game, easily.
61. I will try and hurry up the cleaning.

62. They had ought to tell you where they are going.
63. We walked too school this morning.
64. I should of typed the letter.
65. She likes to sit besides the lamp.
66. I would of done the laundry if you had asked me.
67. Bring your books to the library.
68. They had ought to be spanked.
69. These kind of slacks is popular now.
70. Their family has moved to the city.
71. I took the letter off of the desk.
72. That there girl in the driver's seat is my sister.
73. Mother makes this kind of pizza well.
74. Emily don't know how to make a bed.
75. I shall be happy to except the job.
76. We have all ready completed the test.
77. Please don't be too long at the shopping mall.
78. Don't you think she had ought to invite me, too?
79. I sat besides the child until her mother returned.
80. I looked their, but I couldn't find it.
81. Besides Harry, there were three of us friends at the same camp.
82. There football was run over by a car.
83. Why don't she go to the movies with us?
84. I had ought to go to the dentist for a checkup.
85. You walk to fast, June.
86. We were all together at the time.
87. I learned her to dance this evening.
88. Will you try and be quiet?
89. I belong to this here club.
90. She will let the pupils go home at three o'clock.
91. I like these sort of candies.
92. Dad said he would learn me to play golf.
93. Connie don't look well, does she?
94. This book is different from the one I had last year.
95. Johnny can sing this here song well.
96. I shall write a letter excepting his invitation.
97. Her plane had ought to be taking off soon.
98. Will Mr. Jones leave us go home early today?
99. Bob will try and do better in his grades this year.
100. Although the car was badly damaged, the driver was only slightly injured.

Review of Vocabulary

1. State five ways of building a better vocabulary.
2. Give four uses of words in everyday human activities.
3. Name three principal kinds of information about words that may be found in a standard dictionary.
4. Write three English words related in meaning to these roots:

    a. "port" (carry)   *f.* "vert" (turn)
    b. "scribe" (write)   *g.* "graph" (write)
    c. "dict" (say)   *h.* "ology" (science)
    d. "duct" (lead)   *i.* "phone" (sound)
    e. "spect" (see)   *j.* "chrono" (time)

5. The levels of usage refer to the two chief styles of language:

    a. "__?__" used in formal writing.
    b. "__?__" used in everyday conversation.

6. Faulty diction means __?__.
7. Write correct sentences using these commonly confused words:

    a. accept, except   *f.* can, may
    b. already, all ready   *g.* don't, doesn't
    c. among, between   *h.* learn, teach
    d. beside, besides   *i.* leave, let
    e. bring, take   *j.* there, their

8. Some words are similar in meaning and are called *synonyms*. Words opposite in meaning are called *antonyms*. The dictionary provides many examples of these. Find an appropriate synonym for each word in the first column (*a–j*) below and an antonym for each word in the second column (*k–t*).

    a. ability   *k.* ancient
    b. behavior   *l.* bravery
    c. cheerful   *m.* civilization
    d. decent   *n.* despise
    e. effort   *o.* enlarge
    f. fantastic   *p.* friendship
    g. generous   *q.* gaudy
    h. hopeless   *r.* humorous
    i. identical   *s.* illustrious
    j. lawful   *t.* liberal

Chapter 20

Use the Dictionary
and Other Reference Books

The well-known storywriter O. Henry once said, "If I were shipwrecked on a lonely island, I would like to have two books: a dictionary and the Bible." These two are the best of all reference books for information and inspiration. Make them your companions!

When you enter your school library or the public library, you may find one section set apart for reference only. There you may read but not take home the most useful collection of books. Get acquainted with some of these valuable reference books.

DICTIONARIES

Usually, you look in the dictionary to find the meaning of a word, or the correct spelling, or the acceptable pronunciation. You can also learn the origin of the word, that is, what language it was borrowed from. For example, take this simple sentence:

> After training, the pilot made a *solo* flight.

The word *solo* comes from Italian, originally Latin, *solus* meaning "alone." Thus, you know the pilot took the plane up without an instructor. Furthermore, you can estimate or guess the meaning of a related word *solitary* as in the phrase "solitary confinement."

Every pupil should own and use a dictionary! Some dictionaries recommended for everyday use include:

> *Webster's New Elementary Dictionary*
> *Webster's New Students Dictionary*
> *Thorndike-Barnhart Beginning Dictionary*
> *Thorndike-Barnhart Junior Dictionary*
> *New Winston Dictionary for Young People*
> *Funk & Wagnalls New Standard Dictionary*

ENCYCLOPEDIAS

Sturdy and impressive in their leather bindings, stand several sets of volumes containing a treasury of information. Written by hundreds of experts who specialize in various fields, these books contain articles and pictures about everything in the world, past and present. The articles are arranged in alphabetical order according to topic or subject from AARDVARK to ZYGOTE, or AFGHANISTAN to ZAMBIA.

The word *encyclopedia* means "a complete circle of knowledge." The first set of encyclopedias was prepared by a group of scholars in France during the eighteenth century. The most famous set is the world-renowned *Encyclopaedia Britannica*, especially the eleventh edition published in 1911 and now a collector's item. The most widely used encyclopedias published for youngsters are the following:

The World Book Encyclopedia has twenty-one volumes. It contains numerous articles, pictures, maps, diagrams, and full-length reports on human history and achievement. The topics or subjects are arranged in alphabetical order so that you can locate whatever you need very easily.

Compton's Pictured Encyclopedia has fifteen volumes. In addition to the many factual articles, it contains very interesting excerpts from literature. It is well illustrated in color. Topics relating to general history, science, mathematics, aviation, and other subjects are alphabetically listed.

MISCELLANEOUS REFERENCE BOOKS

A great variety of helpful books deal with every kind of activity in a special way. Here are some examples:

> *The Consumer's Book of Hints & Tips* (household facts)
> *Dictionary of Occupational Titles* (20,000 jobs)
> *Ayer Directory of Publications* (magazines)
> *National ZIP Code and Post Office Directory* (addresses)
> *The World Almanac* (yearbook of facts)
> *Sports Annual* (yearbook of statistics)
> *J. P. Goode's School Atlas* (maps of the world)
> *Columbia Lippincott Gazetteer of the World* (geographical dictionary of countries, cities, rivers, etc.)
> *Bartlett's Familiar Quotations* (famous lines)
> *Betty Betz: Your Manners Are Showing* (etiquette)

Exercises—Reference Books

A. Find the following facts in reference books.

1. Who is the author of *The Divine Comedy*, a famous work describing heaven, hell, and purgatory?
2. Who was the first man to walk on the moon?
3. Who is the scientist who discovered penicillin?
4. During the American Revolutionary War, who was the naval captain who said, "I have not yet begun to fight"?
5. What type of literature did the black author Phillis Wheatley write?
6. Who was the first woman to become Prime Minister of England?
7. In which country did a young Jewish girl write *Anne Frank: The Diary of a Young Girl?*
8. In which country were the Olympic Games originally held?
9. Name the French woman scientist who discovered radium.
10. Stratford-on-Avon was the birthplace of which outstanding English dramatist?

B. Name the reference book you would use to find the answers to these questions.

11. Who was the first president of NOW, the National Organization for Women?
12. Which football team won the Super Bowl for three years in a row?
13. Who won the Women's Singles division of the U.S. Open Tournament in 1980?
14. Who was the first baseball player to beat Babe Ruth's record for home runs in one season?
15. Which city is the capital of Czechoslovakia?
16. What is the ZIP code for the Federal Reserve Bank located in Miami, Florida?
17. Who wrote the following lines?
    "The woods are lovely, dark and deep,
    But I have promises to keep,"
18. Are these magazines still being published—*Fortune, Life, Saturday Evening Post?*
19. What is the best way to clean bathroom tile?
20. What field of service provided Clara Barton an opportunity to help others?

PART FOUR

The Final Score

How well have you learned the essentials? The final test occurs in your everyday use of English in speaking and writing. If you really try to improve yourself, you will.

Keep this book, *Essentials of English,* handy for ready reference. Remember the rule: "When in doubt, look it up!"

TWENTY ACHIEVEMENT TESTS

Some of the following sentences are incorrect and some are correct. Rewrite only those sentences that are incorrect.

Test 1

1. The dog hurt it's paw.
2. Ruth is the more capable of her three sisters.
3. Everyone should do their work well.
4. The lady set down and waited.
5. Please sit besides him.
6. Sarah can swim very well.
7. Dad, can I go with you?
8. I was so frightened I couldn't hardly talk.
9. Rafael is much younger than me.
10. Mother left this for you and I.
11. I can't skate very good.
12. No one suspected that it was me.
13. She didn't have nothing to say.
14. Who's hat is this?
15. The car it is broken.
16. The work was divided among Pablo, Ralph, and me.
17. Have you ate lunch yet?
18. There was an oak tree besides the house.
19. One of those girls are talking too loudly.
20. This is a more easy exercise than the previous one.

Test 2

1. Neither Ann nor Rose have a watch.
2. Walk down the stairs careful.
3. Into which building did he go to?
4. I couldn't find no paper.
5. The teacher scolded Sonya and I.
6. This is the most tallest building I have ever seen.
7. That there house is where I live.
8. John's uncle is very ill.
9. It was him who did the work.
10. Carmelita swum across the lake yesterday.
11. I don't see the brush nowhere.
12. The inks' color is blue.
13. Who are you talking to?
14. My mother she wants me to go home.
15. A stranger come into our school this morning.
16. Frank is the tallest of the two boys.
17. We girls can finish this work before dinner.
18. Every student must do their own lessons.
19. The flowers smell sweetly.
20. Between you and I, he is wrong.

Test 3

1. Nina lay the book on my desk.
2. Lucy is the prettier of the two girls.
3. Her answer is different than mine.
4. This room is their's.
5. It was Sol and me who went.
6. I hope she don't come too early.
7. Neither Henry nor Harry are as capable as Jack.
8. Jacob speaks more rapidly than she.
9. We barely had time to do nothing.
10. The meat tastes badly.
11. He always dresses neat.
12. Either Rosalinda or you is wrong.
13. He is the richest man in town.
14. Bring this book to the office.
15. Who are you writing?
16. May Sheila go, too?
17. I can't see nothing.
18. The childrens' books are here.
19. I received a letter from Mary and she.
20. Have you forgot the wonderful time we had?

Test 4

1. We couldn't scarcely tell the difference.
2. It was him who spoke to the manager of the store.
3. I would like to buy those kind of bikes.
4. Olga doesn't play tennis very well.
5. The bird broke it's wing.
6. She always done her work well.
7. He learned me to play the piano.
8. Sam is a more better singer than Joe.
9. Everyone must bring a letter from their parents.
10. There was some confusion between Leon and I.
11. Is this pencil your's?
12. Mae is older than me.
13. The cake looks deliciously.
14. Renée prefers this kind of hat.
15. She has knew me for three years.
16. Leave it go.
17. These are the most beautifullest flowers in the store.
18. She said she hadn't no time.
19. This book of poems are very interesting.
20. Mother called both you and me.

Test 5

1. Don't you want to set here beside me?
2. Marietta should of reminded me.
3. Mother spoke about Lewis and he.
4. The situation was such that I couldn't say nothing.
5. Ralph is the least studious of Mrs. Lane's two children.
6. I looked their but didn't find it.
7. Who's racket did you use?
8. Always cross the streets carefully.
9. Either John or the girls is going to stay home.
10. There is no doubt that it was her who called.
11. Rose is more stronger than Violet.
12. I was too sleepy to talk to them.
13. Take this off of the desk.
14. Tell me who you are writing.
15. We barely had room to do anything.
16. Concetta said she would try and come to the party.
17. She doesn't play the piano very good.
18. Every one of the boys know you cheated.
19. Father has often spoken of Miriam and she.
20. Do you know who lay those books on the floor?

Test 6

1. I doubt that she has went to school.
2. This here boy is my best friend.
3. The crate of oranges have come.
4. The knife don't appear sharp.
5. Either you or Carla are responsible for this accident.
6. He was in such a hurry he didn't hardly eat.
7. Army life is different than civilian life.
8. She said I don't dance very well.
9. My teacher she was absent today.
10. Josephine is smarter than I.
11. These exercises are not two difficult, are they?
12. It was him who broke the glass.
13. I doubt that you done your best.
14. Aunt Maggie persuaded Dad to leave us go to the party.
15. My father is a more smarter man than yours.
16. Either Lucille or Michelle left their books.
17. After the rain, my hat lost it's shape.
18. Mother, can I go to the game Saturday?
19. Were you cautioned to cross the streets carefully?
20. Try and talk to Joe tonight.

Test 7

1. Every student passed their test.
2. This work is to be divided between you and I.
3. The pencil was broke, so I couldn't write.
4. No one could of done better work.
5. She is the younger of the two sisters.
6. We were asked to set the books on the table.
7. You had ought to tell Dad.
8. To whom are you waving?
9. We couldn't do nothing for her.
10. He placed the chair besides the wall.
11. She must of been very excited over the news.
12. Have you wrote your lessons in ink?
13. Can I go, too?
14. I couldn't find my hat nowhere.
15. I like Lou's watch, but not your's.
16. Do you think I should let her go out in this rain?
17. The same gift was sent to Sylvia and she.
18. Neither you nor she are going.
19. Your coat is different than mine.
20. One of the men were here today.

Test 8

1. Neither Jacqueline nor the twins is at school.
2. Don't it look like rain?
3. Who's gloves are these?
4. The boys rode there bikes to school.
5. It was him who write the letter.
6. Has Bernardine drunk all the milk?
7. You may of seen him.
8. She gave me some cake that tasted very richly.
9. One of my friends is here.
10. That there dog is Frank's.
11. Ricardo he is sick with the measles.
12. Between you and I, I think Henry is wrong.
13. Colleen come home yesterday.
14. We could of finished before dinner.
15. I was hungry and the dinner looked very appetizing.
16. She had ought to confide in her mother.
17. This assortment of candies are excellent.
18. Terry's answer is different than ours.
19. My sister is more taller than yours.
20. Bring this chair to the next room.

Test 9

1. Helen asked me to try and call him.
2. You write too jerkily.
3. The boy's were taught wrestling.
4. Hector and Gabriel brought there skates with them.
5. The bottle had fell from the table.
6. This is the more interesting of the two books.
7. Why don't she help you?
8. We boys went to the meeting altogether.
9. He is entirely two careless in his work.
10. Is there enough room for Sophie and I?
11. Can I take the dog for a walk?
12. I want each of you boys to memorize their speech.
13. I tried to move the trunk but it was to heavy.
14. For her to do such a thing is a surprise.
15. Johns' brother is a Marine.
16. Mother laid in bed for a while and felt better.
17. To whom are you going to write to?
18. It was so warm we couldn't hardly do any work.
19. What type of car has your father bought?
20. This is the most carefully written letter of all.

Test 10

1. Either the boys or the girls is to use the gym.
2. My two brothers sold their cars.
3. They have went to Antonia's house and not yours.
4. Norma learned me how to swim.
5. This here watch is a very good one.
6. I don't believe the box of eggs are broken.
7. I like these sort of sweaters.
8. I believe this letter was written by either you or she.
9. Mary is different than most of the other girls.
10. Ellen she told me she wants to see you.
11. He parked the car besides the house.
12. No one doubts it is she.
13. Walter is the least ambitious of the two boys.
14. It was divided between Dora, Flossie, and me.
15. Who's sweater did you lay on the floor?
16. Either you or Rodney is to go to the store.
17. You had ought to stay in bed until you feel better.
18. We were teached the parts of speech.
19. It's a certainty that the horse broke it's leg.
20. We would of been happy to go.

Test 11

1. Is she taller than I?
2. You should of been home this afternoon.
3. I remember that I had went to school without my pen.
4. The tea tastes sweetly.
5. She did not have nothing to do.
6. Our new dog it is very young.
7. Which I liked very much.
8. Who's jacket is this?
9. Laura will be transferred to western high school, Father said.
10. Neither one have been to a ball game this season.
11. Set beside the fireplace and dry your clothes.
12. Let's meet at Judy's house tonight and visit Edith all together.
13. Everyone should talk to their parents.
14. They couldn't hardly tell the difference between them.
15. Hoping to see you after school.
16. While walking to school with Peter Jack Tom and Robert I suggested that we boys go to the movies in the afternoon.
17. Don't she want to go?
18. My aunt left it for you and I.
19. Mr. Ripple said that I am the less studious boy in the class.
20. The poor man refuses to accept charity; he says he is looking for a job.

Test 12

1. Can I take this book home?
2. Who did you write to?
3. I would of hurried if I had known.
4. Do these eggs smell badly to you?
5. That there purse is her's.
6. Between you and me, perhaps he is wrong.
7. We seen many pretty dresses at Macy's.
8. The postal service loses money delivering "junk" mail.
9. No one was home, I was lonesome.
10. Each of them were very talkative.
11. Us children always help with the dishes.
12. I wrote the letter very neat and carefully.
13. I have always did my best work.
14. We found our books but their's are lost.
15. The trunk was two heavy to carry; so we pushed it beside the wall.
16. Your dog is more friendlier than mine.
17. Which no sane person would do.
18. How many want to join the Red Cross? Mrs Taylor asked.
19. Margaret, don't you know Lila's last name?
20. The woman who spoke to you and I is Miss Ross.

Test 13

1. I went home early, I did not feel well.
2. Either Clarence or Wallace are at fault.
3. The loser is she, but she won't admit it.
4. Lets go to Jacks house for a while.
5. The address of cleveland college is 14 west roosevelt avenue.
6. Ted must of been happy to see you.
7. She is besides the car waiting for you.
8. Miss Haskins left a note for Becky and I.
9. I haven't any work to do today.
10. Robert has took the box of candy.
11. We were already to go out when it started to rain.
12. You are smarter than her.
13. Neither Margie nor the boys is home.
14. Dont swim out too far Dad shouted.
15. Mr. Raymond's horse broke it's leg.
16. That she said was true.
17. What kind of a car does your aunt have?
18. Harold said that I should have did better.
19. We have a cat and two dogs, a terrier and a bull.
20. The dog laid in front of the door and fell asleep.

Test 14

1. The box of eggs are on the table.
2. There is Tom's father, he is a doctor.
3. The siren frightened we children.
4. You should of asked your neighbor's permission.
5. According to the *new york times* new york had more rain in september than in july or august.
6. Whom do you think I spoke to today?
7. Bring these books upstairs.
8. Mother sent me for tomatos, potatos, and two loafs of bread.
9. Do you think she plays the piano very good?
10. Her answer is different than mine.
11. He sat the book on my desk.
12. Dans' sweater is lost.
13. The lunch was divided between Victor and I.
14. Neither Lucy nor the twins play the piano.
15. One of my brothers was married last sunday.
16. Mr. Smith gave her and he some advice.
17. Have you met our new neighbors the people who own the diner?
18. The bottle fell on the floor and breaked.
19. It is she who is collecting seashells.
20. He always done his work quickly and accurately, he was a good student.

Test 15

1. Won't you come with we girls?
2. The reason being that I have few friends.
3. My sister she bought a new ring.
4. Neither Joe nor Benny are so strong as I.
5. "Please leave the room," said the teacher.
6. Doesnt he need money Mother asked.
7. Dad wants to take you and she for a walk.
8. This is all together too sudden.
9. We were asked to lie our work aside for a while.
10. Who's offer will you accept?
11. The heroe's deeds were known even by his enemys.
12. It was me who wrote the letter.
13. My friend learned me to dance.
14. Among the groups of girls, I like ours best.
15. Either you or they is to help me.
16. Bring this report to the principal's office.
17. My dog blackie was found on rose street.
18. The violin does not sound well.
19. This is the more better of the two.
20. I bought a baseball glove, it is a birthday gift for my friend Vincent.

Test 16

1. I laid the book in its proper place.
2. Each of the children carried their lunch.
3. May Sid and I go to the movies, Mother?
4. Let's walk home, it's only a half mile.
5. At that distance we couldn't see nothing.
6. Kate locate the Sahara Desert the Mediterranean Sea and the Atlantic Ocean.
7. Miss Trask invited Ronald and I to her home.
8. The ladys are in the park watching their babys.
9. My sister teached me to swim.
10. May us girls go with Dave to the beach?
11. The box of cookies are for you and me.
12. Have you ate your lunch?
13. Sorry we must leave so soon.
14. He don't know the answer, but I do.
15. The mens' team played the womens' team.
16. No one could have played the part better than him.
17. The butterfly broke it's wing.
18. Our new teacher is different than the others.
19. Beside Rita, there are three in my family.
20. Sam, Jack, and I went for a hike on Sunday.

Test 17

1. Have you wrote to Elizabeth?
2. Who is he? He looks familiar.
3. My brothers' new watch was stolen.
4. Emma is the more livelier of the two girls.
5. Ask your mother if she will leave you go to the movies with me.
6. What kind of game do you call this?
7. Every student was asked to do their best.
8. Always speak distinct.
9. Can I go with you, Paul?
10. As Lena has so often said.
11. Anne, May, and me are going to Uncle Jim's store.
12. When we couldn't find our way home.
13. You had ought to study harder if you wish to pass the test.
14. Who's going to the Masque Club's ball?
15. Because she could not see her father before he went to work.
16. What did you ate for dinner?
17. Besides me there are four of us going to the game.
18. Please try and come to my party.
19. Why don't he swim so well as you and I?
20. This crate of oranges are from Florida.

Test 18

1. Who did you call this afternoon?
2. I am trying to learn how to ski.
3. It was so noisy, you could barely hear your own voice.
4. The dentist taught the students how to brush their teeth.
5. Is it alright if I go home now?
6. Many in the class brought they're dictionary.
7. Dad drove my sister and me to school.
8. Hoping you will come Saturday.
9. Of my many friends, Sal is the loyalest.
10. Take the dishes off of the table.
11. She looked beautifully in her new clothes.
12. It's him who broke the radio.
13. Everyone played his or her part well.
14. In the country we saw some ponies, oxen, calves, and sheep.
15. He laid on the couch and sobbed.
16. I wanted to get into the movies. But it was too crowded.
17. This pencil it doesn't write.
18. What kind of a book do you want?
19. This here pen is broken.
20. At the next meeting, us club members will vote for new officers.

Test 19

1. You know where Anthony lives, you should not get lost.
2. How are you Al Smitty shouted.
3. Who's mistake is it?
4. The cat drunk all the milk in the pan.
5. George, Harold, and me went to the skating rink.
6. That girl young and talented.
7. We came home wet and cold, but not too tired to eat.
8. Neither Juanita nor Mary were asked to the party.
9. One of the trees beside our house are oak.
10. That there house is theirs.
11. Has Benjamin drank his milk?
12. My homework assignment was two difficult.
13. Ken's father is not attending the meeting but ours is.
14. Do you think Hugo plays checkers better than me?
15. I forgot my watch, I don't know what time it is.
16. Miss Jones my neighbor gave me treasure island david copperfield and huckleberry finn.
17. Lets go to the museum on Saturday.
18. It is I who called Aunt Molly.
19. The perfume she uses smells sweetly.
20. We couldn't do nothing but rest.

Test 20

1. One of the players sprained their wrist.
2. Father took Helen, Catherine, and she on a picnic.
3. Doesn't the car look cleanly after the wash?
4. Alex is the younger of the two boys.
5. You know the rules, don't break them.
6. The mens' team is practicing in the gym.
7. We run all the way to school this morning.
8. Please lie the packages on the table and set down for a while.
9. The bundle of papers were burned in the furnace.
10. You had ought to do better work in school.
11. Everyone except Ann are to go home.
12. Will you join we boys in a game of tennis?
13. The crowd whistling and cheering.
14. It's a certainty that the horse beat its previous record.
15. Why dont he write me more frequently she asked.
16. I can't go nowhere, for I am waiting to see my mother.
17. Lets go to the main street theater the new one where big shot is playing.
18. Catherine has just went out.
19. There is something wrong with this butter; it smells badly.
20. Who did you speak to on the telephone?

Index

215

sentences:
definition, 5
parts of sentences, 5–12
building sentences, 11, 24–25
kinds of sentences, 13, 17
combining sentences, 19
sentence patterns, 21, 24–25
faulty sentences, 25–27
writing better sentences, 28–29
incomplete sentences, 31–32
sentence errors to avoid, 31–34
sequence of tenses, 86–87
simple sentences, 17
simple subjects, 7
skimpy sentences, 25
spelling, 135–144
standard and nonstandard English, 1, 193
state-of-being (linking) verbs, 78, 103
subject:
subject and verb in sentences, 7–8, 9,
88–91
noun used as subject, 47
agreement with verb, 55–56, 88–91
subordinate (dependent) clauses, 14–15,
17
subordinate conjunctions, 15, 124
suffixes, 147, 151

tense, 80–87

usage, definition, 38

verbs:
subject and verb in sentences, 7–8, 9,
88–91
predicate verbs, 7
verb phrases, 7, 79
complements of verbs, 22–23
action verbs, 22, 78
linking (state-of-being) verbs, 22, 78,
101
definition, 40, 75, 78–79
main verbs, 78, 79
helping verbs, 79
tense of verbs, 79–83, 85–87
regular and irregular verbs, 80–81
principal parts of verbs, 81–83
agreement of subject and verb, 55–56,
88–91
endings of verbs, 93
verbs of the senses, 103
vocabulary, 178–197
vowels, 50

who, whom, case of, 65
writing better sentences, 28–29
wrong connections in sentences, 26